COUNTRY DAYS
A Childhood Remembered

Ken Pickford

PETER WATTS
Publishing

Published in Great Britain by
Peter Watts Publishing Ltd
13-15 Stroud Road
Gloucester, GL1 5AA

ISBN 0 906025 59 1 [case]
ISBN 0 906025 60 5 [limp]

Typesetting and Artwork by
Senior Publications, Glossop, Derbyshire

Printed and bound by
Mather Brothers [Printers] Ltd, Preston

Facing page: Present day Standish Court.   [Michael Edmonds]

Contents

The Pickford family portrait
featuring the author
[aged five] and his father,
mother and sister.

Foreword

Having now lived the greater part of my life, I have looked back over the years and decided that the time I most enjoyed was that between the age of six and ten. These were the days of long hot summers — the period before living became a responsibility.

I have amused myself by setting down on paper those things which I vividly remember happening in these days of youthful innocence. Here is the record as truthfully as my memory serves, complete with real 'colourful' characters; and I trust that in no way have I been guilty of derogation. These people make the record absolutely correct and I know they would not wish me to give them false names.

It is now over sixty years since Standish Court was my country home and a lot of changes, good and bad, have affected our environment and way of life. I only hope that present ten-year-olds can still enjoy the sense of elation which I experienced at their age.

I hope that you will enjoy reading this little book.

Sheepscombe, Glos.   K. D. P. Pickford

Chapter one
'The big'un furst'

I first remember a wonderful blue object which was rolled into my small clammy hand by the grimy thumb and forefinger of a thieving accomplice. Had I been given an oriental jewel by the Thief of Baghdad I could not have experienced a more sudden joy. This new treasure mirrored the summer sunshine with a milky reflection and yet was itself brighter than the cloudless sky above. Never before had my juvenile eyes seen anything more beautiful. I resisted the temptation to pop it into my mouth with some difficulty, because at this tender toddling age I had not quite overcome the desire which came to me with my birth. It was still my habit to suck things, particularly if they were round and small.

I stood in my neat little smock and sandals, my hands cupped one above the other, dwarfed by the bony youth who had just emerged from the dense brushwood surrounding a country churchyard yew.

"It's an 'edge sparrer's egg," I was told, "and mind 'e don't break 'un!"

Sam Harris was cowman's boy at Standish and was himself just old enough to do odd jobs and run errands, although in those far off days children, through necessity, were often pressed into service at a tender age. Sam was the last of a line of thirteen children beget by Ephraim and Clara and, maybe because of this doubtful fortune, escaped the rigours experienced by his elder brethren. He was, nevertheless, a ragged mortal and wore a coat, shirt and trousers which had long since been discarded by a grown-up near twice his size. The black serge suit had lost its waistcoat and was also lacking

5

sizeable portions of cloth at pocket and buttock. Some of this still hung in garlands and awkward shapes around his person and exposed the grubby yellow patching of his underclothing. Projecting from his one good pocket was a red handkerchief with white spots — the badge of a true countryman. This square of coloured cloth served purpose to carry chunks of bread, wipe cider from grizzled whiskers and, when knotted at the corners, protected the bald pate from the sun in hay and harvest field.

Sam was sallow and when he grinned at my pleasure he exposed a row of yellow teeth to show the warm affection he held for me. For several weeks previous, he had been by almost constant companion, for I had been handed into his safe daytime charge by my grandmother, who was farmer's wife at Standish Court.

"Young Ken will be alright with Sam," she had said; and from that very moment I had begun to experience the unfettered joy of being a country bumpkin.

The family doctor had decided that I was somewhat delicate and that I would do well to run wild on the farm for the summer. A kinder prescription I have yet to experience. For four tender years such existence had remained a dormant desire in my veins and when my mother delivered me back to the earthy heritage which had been her maiden home, my puny body reacted as a wilting cabbage plunged into water.

Earlier expeditions with Sam had given me my first real taste of the country. Wild rabbits, with their bobbing white tails, delighted me when I chased them on close-cropped Court Hill, which they infested. They did not appear unduly perturbed at my efforts, keeping always that safe distance in front, and I could never quite catch up with them before they flicked into their burrows. I had plunged and splashed my bare legs in the sparkling brook that eddied through the farm and I had watched the baby trout dart away to cover. Splashing was wonderful fun, only to be discontinued when the ice-cold water ran along my legs, percolating my pants and the grassy bank on which I sat.

I had learnt the joy of being hoisted on to the broad expansive back of Duke, the pride of the stables. He was a massive creature who thrilled and yet frightened me. Clinging precariously to the brightly shining harness that adorned my lofty platform, I remember the exciting sensation of instability as Duke ambled across the meadows. Great muscles bunched under his slick hairy pelt and rippled warm to my bare yielding knees. If I rubbed that bright chestnut coat of his then my small hands shone with oily graphite and smelt satisfactorily musty. When the strong arms of the carter lowered me to the ground at the end of my ride I felt that I had been yet further reduced in size.

I had picked wild flowers, rolled in the moist warm grass, been stung by a wasp and bitten by a ferret. I had learnt also the wonder of splashing in muddy puddles and getting the good dark earth on my arms and legs, now well scratched and browned by the sun. All this and more had been my joy during the early carefree days of freedom; but now I was being permitted to take part in an adventure which sent my heart pounding with excitement. Rude awakenings were in embryo in that country churchyard and I was taking my first step to becoming a part of nature's ruthless pattern.

Standish churchyard.   [Michael Edmonds]

Sam and I followed the winding path through the tomb-stones and passed through the Gothic door into the Court gardens, neat-bordered with dwarf box hedging. We paused a few moments with Maurice Underwood, the gardener, who stood splay-legged, the handle of his hoe pushing a hole under his chin.

"Now wat 'av you young scamps bin at? Bird nestin' I'll be bound," said Maurice, as I proudly pushed my hands, still cuppoed, upwards towards his face. "Y'd better get Sam to blow 'un afore 'e gets broke."

I was wisely instructed, but as yet such technical matters were to me unknown and my only desire was that I should show my new treasure to the family indoors.

We were met at the back door to the kitchen by my Aunt Emily. She quickly appreciated the importance of the whole affair and decided that a safe storage must immediately be found to secure so valuable a possession. There could be no other place than inside the silk embroidered tea cosy. This was used only on very special occasions and would remain un-touched by anyone save my aunt until someone married, died, or it was Christmas.

Sam and I followed Aunt Emily to the china cupboard. Befitting its quality, the best tableware was kept separately in a cabinet which had curved mahogany doors. Inside, a pleated red satin lining produced a rosy mirror in the well-polished glass front. Here was assembled the family Wedgewood and Spode. Lying on its side on a middle shelf rested the tea cosy, a work of exquisite skill and patience. It was quilted, tasselled, and profusely lined with cotton-wool padding. Quite a proper receptacle for my equally priceless possession, I thought. My little blue sparrow egg was duly inserted into the womb of silk and satin where it remained intact for a surprisingly long time.

It was, of course, frequently removed for exhibition, in turn, to my three uncles, to Mr Cull the grocer, to Mr Aldridge who came to buy the great cheeses produced by my grand-mother, and to any other person I thought worthy of the honour.

My aunt's assistance was enlisted on such occasions, but I soon discovered that a tall wooden chair in the kitchen would permit me to carry out the operation for myself. By clambering up onto the chair I could just reach the requisite shelf. Inspections became more and more frequent but alas, on one such occasion the inevitable happened; the chair slipped and the egg fell from my over-anxious fingers. Only a sticky yellow blob with a halo of blue on the flag-stone floor below made me aware of the tragic reality. For a few moments I stood motionless, then the silken oyster followed its pearl to the floor and I sagged slightly as the knees. Slowly my shocked and pallid face wrinkled near the eyes, my mouth opened, and I howled and howled and howled.

This sad and sudden calamity was fully appreciated by all members of the family who strove valiantly to alleviate my dejection. Special favours were bestowed upon me in an abortive attempt to distract my attention. My snivelling nostrils were suffocated in several bosoms and I was petted and pampered by the menfolk. With a knowing nod to my grandmother, Aunt Emily disappeared upstairs to her bedroom and returned with a tiny drawer from her dressing table. This contained numerous beads, brightly coloured and variagated, the residue of several necklaces awaiting the opportune moment for re-threading. The hoarded treasure was tipped with abandon onto the maroon chenille tablecloth before my very eyes — but I would have none of it. This subtle attempt to provide substitution misfired completely because it only served to remind me of the loss, and I redoubled efforts to spread my misery to ears even further afield.

Outside in a yard, one of the dairy herd was bemoaning the loss of a calf, sent to market that morning. I, at least, appeared to be attracting the greater sympathy. It will never be known, of course, which of the two of us, the shorthorn or I, first regained normality, but in my own case the worst pangs were over by the next morning. However, both the cow and I gave vent to our misery during the closing hour of day.

When the morning came, I was at last brightened by the

prospect that it was time to feed the poultry. This I found to be a highly satisfactory experience, being allowed to take a major hand in the operation. The feeding I did entirely on my own, but my aunt still insisted that she should carry the very large bucket whch was three-parts filled with Indian corn. There was, of course, a serious risk that otherwise I would spill the grain before we arrived in the commodious rick-yard where stood a number of poultry houses. I had learnt, quite quickly, that it was necessary to throw the corn around in a wide arc and that, at the same time, stimulating noises should be made: "Cum on, chick, chick, chick." If the ducks and geese were tardy in coming from the stream, then the call should be varied to, "Dill, dill, dill."

Of course, I had developed feeding variations and techniques of my own, but they were not all approved by Aunt Emily. A little old saucepan was used to bail the corn from the bucket and I had found that this would make satisfactory trails of grain which could be laid, at will, in any direction. By squatting at the end of a trail, a confiding old hen could be grabbed. Sometimes she would squawk and flutter with surprising power and, ultimately would have to be released. On other occasions she would immediately crouch close to the ground, arch her wings and wait. I could not understand why she should be so submissive but, in this stupefied condition, could easily be picked up and planted on my knee. Here she would stand for a few moments, quite motionless, with beak partly open, eyes glaring and crop muscles convulsing. When her sexual impulse was once again outweighed by that of hunger, she would suddenly spring to the ground and continue gobbling the grain.

The little golden corns themselves fascinated me. It was surprising how fast a handful of them could be devoured, one at a time, by a tame member of the flock. I loved the sensation of the vibrating beak hammering at my palm and was amused when the hand-reared glutton choked and gasped for breath.

Whilst I was distributing the food, in not always equal shares, my aunt made her routine visits to the nesting boxes.

When she returned to me, I was informed that one of my ducks had stolen a nest. Here I must explain that there were four small mallard ducks which fed with the poultry and whose origin was the discovered nest of a wild bird. An obliging broody hen had completed the task of incubation in a small wooden coop and her foster children had grown up in a state of semi-captivity. It was natural enough that, when told the story, I should claim the orphans as my property and that I should endeavour to ensure that they had a fair share of the corn. Matters of nidification were beyond me at this early stage but my aunt was well informed.

"We must get a ladder," she said, "and search the tops of all the hay and corn stacks in the yard." Accordingly, we repaired to the wagon-shed where a number of ladders were stored on top of the low wooden beams. I loved this old building because it contained so many wonderful things. It never failed to stimulate my ready imagination.

Several great wagons stood shoulder to shoulder, bearing my grandfather's name on their breast-plates. They were the heavy brigade in every engagement, trundling out at my grandfather's command with teams of horses and men to win the harvest from the land and return laden with spoils of conquest. Their massive wheels, iron shod, turned on a camber from the axle so that they might better support the heavy loads thrust upon them. Though they creaked and groaned they never yielded and, like the stone building in which they stood, were handed down from generation to generation with little need for repair. Very soon they would be in motion again because, even now, the cutters were at work in the hayfield.

It was, however, to my aunt's detriment that the season was a little late. The wagon immediately below the ladder she had selected for our purpose was thick with dust and the droppings from the poultry; but to country people such hazards are commonplace. With the aid of an old broom she soon cleared a pathway to her objective. Once attained, the ladder was slid away from its resting place and the search began. We clambered boisterously atop hay and straw and, when our first efforts came to naught, we probed the crowns of the pollarded willows against the stream. It was all without avail so when at last the ladder was returned to its oaken anchorage, the mallard nest remained undiscovered.

"We are a bright pair, aren't we?" said Aunt Emily. "Fancy letting a little duck lay all those eggs and not be able to find them."

For my part, I found this hypothesis most confusing. My mind was not capable of reason beyond the positive and I could not understand how my aunt could be so sure. Like most children, however, I was prepared to believe, without question, any person I trusted. And I trusted Aunt Emily.

For most of the time during the remainder of the day I pondered on my little duck and its nest. In fact it was never really out of my thoughts. Even when I curled up in bed with the daylight still shining through the lace curtains at the lattice windows, my problem was still with me.

The broad old four-poster, with a small human indentation deep in its cosy feather underlay, carried me away to my dreams. The now familiar objects in the bedroom faded with my oblivion and I was, once again, holding the little saucepan with the milling flock all around. One of the little mallard ducks was missing, of that I was certain, and I knew that it would come to me if I called.

Looking upwards and around, I shouted clearly, "Cum on, dill, dill, dill."

In immediate response, a flurry of wings descended to my feet and in my dreams I had discovered the nest.

Awaking early next morning I made all haste to tell Aunt Emily, and so certain was I that my dream would come true, persuaded her to abandon breakfast and follow me.

When we arrived in the rick-yard, complete with a hastily gathered supply of corn, I quickly pointed out the position of the nest.

"Tis on that wall," I asserted.

My aunt was obviously by now taking me quite seriously because she made away to collect the ladder whilst I stood gleefully awaiting the result of her inspection.

The stone wall, about eight feet high, formed a boundary to the garden and, for a stretch of its length, was capped with a Virginia creeper which had roots on the cultivated side. It was into this leafy tangle that the crop of the ladder was pushed . . . . . . and away flew the little mallard duck.

I can offer no explanation of course. It would be futile for me to claim that my dreams often come true, because this is not the case. However, I felt that my standing went up appreciably with the carter and the cowman when the story was recounted to them. This gave me great satisfaction!

This new excitement obliterated my earlier dejection, particularly when I was allowed to examine the nest when the duck came off to feed later in the day. Climbing gingerly up the ladder, with my aunt behind, her body acting as a guard-rail, I peeped down through the glossy leaves of the tangling creeper. There, in a natural crevice on top of the wall, was the beautifully soft nest. The down was partly covering the eggs, and, although I was not competent to count them for myself, was told that there were thirteen in all.

Without reference to the laws of fertility, I remember that I immediately decided that Sam and his brothers and sisters should be given a duckling each when the eggs hatched. My aunt quickly accepted this suggestion and promptly christened my little nesting duck Clara Harris the Second. Unfortunately, I was not destined to be present when the hatching took place because I was collected from Standish by my mother and returned to our house in the town to greet my father upon his homecoming 'on leave' from the War.

My poor father was, to me, a stranger with a very red face, for he had departed 'to the front' before I could toddle. Now, to celebrate his safe return, there was to be a great reunion among my father's people, from near and far, at my Uncle Harry's house. I was told that I must be on my very best behaviour, but as I had no particular desire to be away from the fields and the sunshine it is to my discredit that I caused mother much concern whilst being scrubbed and dressed for the affair. Father fed me a good supply of chocolate bars which he had brought home and the preparations continued.

At last, with face shining, hair well brushed and a lace collar separating my head from a new velvet suit, I was introduced to the guests assembled at Uncle Harry's. There followed a period of anxiety for my mother, during which I was picked up and put down, kissed, prodded, bushy whiskers thrust into my face and finally speared with a wax moustache. When all was over without calamity, I was turned loose in the yard with my cousin, Glyn, so that we might play quietly together.

Later, we were called in for a meal, but it was I alone who answered. Questions were asked concerning Glyn's whereabouts and I countered with some reluctance, "I've shut 'un up along a th' cows."

The unfortunate Glyn was soon released from behind the locked door of an outside lavatory.

This little escapade received only a mixed reception and we settled ourselves at the table. The assembled company comprised some ten or twelve persons. Uncle Harry, having made great sport of sharpening his carving knife, commenced a series of attacks on the carcass of a plump roasted chicken.

Serving was done by family seniority, even to the extent that the carver served himself before attending to the wants of the children. I watched the chicken frame yield most of its meat, and the sausages, which had originally surrounded it in goodly numbers, reduce by twos and threes.

Glyn was the penultimate to receive attention and when it came to my turn two sausages only remained. Having discovered a few lurking pieces of meat which had escaped previous attention, my uncle looked down at me before proceeding further, the knife still poised in his right hand and the fork, in the left, gyrating over the sausages.

"Now, my little man," he said, "which of these do you think you can manage? Should I give you the large one or will the small one be sufficient?"

My answer and country appetite was sharp enough because I quickly replied, "I'll 'ave th' big 'un furst an' th' little 'un

14

arder.''

The company was greatly amused and laughed heartily at my ready answer, but I apprehended an atmosphere of mild contempt among a few of my relatives. I was doubtless fast becoming a yokel and I am certain that they were prepared to consider me irretrievably lost to sophisticated society. At all events, I was sublimely indifferent to my newly acquired dialect and quite unabashed that I should be creating an unfavourable impression.

Glyn and I were packed off to bed at our normal early hour and so I did not completely ruin my reputation. The grown-ups obviously continued their celebrations long after I was fast asleep and I have no knowledge of how I found my way into my own bed at home. I presume that I was wrapped in a blanket and conveyed there in a torpid condition during the night because I was still wearing my socks and underclothing when I awoke next morning.

Soon after waking, my mother entered the bedroom declaring that it had been decided that I should return to Standish later in the day. With this good news I submitted more eagerly than usual to my ablutions and then dressed, with father fastening up my sandals. He was proving himself less and less frightening, for the rough khaki suiting which made my face sore had now been shed and he was wearing clothes to which I was more accustomed. His face appeared even redder above a white starched collar, but his eyes were kind.

When all was ready, and the breakfast things cleared away, father busied himself securing the house. He carried the bags down from upstairs and collected our coats from the pegs in the hall. In fact, he seemed to be doing a lot of things which had hitherto been my mother's sole prerogative. She easily accepted the new situation, appearing sublimely happy that this still rather strange man should be wanting to do things for us. On the other hand, my gurgling baby sister remained aloof in my mother's arms oblivious of the fact that our little family had now become four.

We trooped down the garden path and boarded a clunking

[Top] Gloucester City Corporation trams Nos. 2 and 4 stand at St. Barnabas, Tuffley. [Courtesy R. A. Jordan]

[Above] Haresfield station in the days of steam. The platforms only served the LMS lines, not the Great Western. [Courtesy Mrs J. Thomas]

tramcar which ground and squirmed us along its shallow rails to the middle of the town. Here, after much clatter and bustle, a steam train was boarded at Gloucester Eastgate station which would carry us through the green fields to Haresfield.

The journey was short and soon we were tumbling with our baggage from the smoke-filled carriage. We walked along the narrow echoing platform and down a ramp to the crossing-gates. Here, through the stout wire mesh, I caught a glimpse of old George Hughes, the carter from the Court.

George had his back to us and his bare brown arm was securing the frothy bit of a frightened blinkered pony. The lower half of an unbuttoned shirt sleeve flagged downwards from his elbow, whilst that on the other arm, tightly rolled, bunched a biceps as big as a goose egg. His broad sleek back grew out of the funnelled top of a pair of corduroy trousers, and somewhere below his middle, a loose shiny leather belt, brass studded, swept downwards towards the front to support his ample belly. The legs of his trousers were hitched at the knees with string to expose the full extent ot a pair of heavy hobnailed boots. Standish boasted no coachman, but what George lacked in appearance he matched with a canny under-standing of his horses.

When the last rumblings of the departing train had died away we loaded ourselves into the conveyance and 'clip-clopped' away from the station. In the trap behind the pony my grand-mother and Aunt Emily bounced with the oscillations, their broad-brimmed hats secured with muslin scarves, playing havoc with their bunched-up hair.

We were a very full load but there was plenty of time and only a mile or two in front of us. The way lay along a narrow winding lane which was still virgin to a motor-car.

It was a lovely day, soft and still. Brown butterflies flicked above the tall grasses on the road verge and busy bees were obtaining their clammy reward from the wild flowers growing in profusion. Skeins of gnats danced in the shadows of the haw-thorn, dipping in pairs to the stagnant water in the ditches. Overhead, hazel curved in graceful arching and was crowned by the great elms which stretched their mighty arms in leafy splendour.

The quietly trotting pony jerked us along with an easy motion as the metal-clad wheels ground the grit on the road below. At sometime on our journey old Dobbin twitched and lifted his tail and George Hughes slackened speed to accommodate. Even in such earthy matters, horse and man understood each other. The little steaming balls were left at regular intervals among the tufts of grass which clung to the middle of the road. Occasionally, we ducked our heads to pass underneath a particularly low branch, and once the carter broke off the offending limb, tossing it down to where the verge was widest.

All too soon we emerged from the leafy canopy and swung left into the open of the Stonehouse road. Here, great fields stretched away on either side and we had our first glimpse of the slender spire of Standish Church. It was not long before we were passing under the great stone archway which, it is said, had years before stood sentinel over the body of foul murdered Edward the Second from Berkeley. Now, crumbling, it marked the end of the drive to the Court. This was Standish. Standish of my many childhood memories. The great stone pile mellow in the afternoon sun with pear and creeper reaching up on its homely walls. The flag-stoned inner yard and the iron-studded door.

I was back again and life for me was at its beginning.

Standish Court archway.   **[Michael Edmonds]**

18

Standish church.   [Michael Edmonds]

Chapter two
Sweet summer

When my father decided to remain at Standish for a few days, Sam and I found a new companion who easily shared our friendship. It was quite a new experience to discover a 'grown-up' who was prepared to do all those things which appealed to us and to enjoy them as much as we did. My uncles, each and every one, had always been most helpful and would answer my many questions with considerable patience, but they were mostly busy and could spare only limited time. Father, on the other hand, did not tire and was always thinking of something new to do. He, it was, who decided that we should go fishing.

The brook which ran through the farm was quite small and for most of its length it was shallow. There were, however, little pools and eddies and man-made deeper places where the water was placid. My father, as if by magic, produced from his pockets a packet of fishing hooks and a skein of line. He clambered up into a willow and hacked off three stout branches with his knife. Sam had almost stripped the first of its leaves before the second crashed to the ground and soon the trusty rods took shape.

"Ye ken cut I a dozen er two ov they," smiled Maurice Underwood. "They 'ill do fer next yer's beans, I be short alreddie."

But of course the gardener knew his suggestion would make little impression and so he added, "Done lop 'un off too short, Sam, theese wans 'en long enuf fer ter reach the middle." Sam just grinned back at him without answering. He had fished many times before and needed no instruction.

As if to prove his knowledge, he cut a small groove around all three rods almost at the slender end to retain the lines and wound each round several times before making the knot. Floats were made from bottle corks, partly split through and holed from top to bottom with a quill. When the hooks were attached everything was complete. My line was baited for me with a big red worm which fell into the middle of the stream with a 'plop', the rod was laid through the rushes and I was directed to watch carefully. Sam and my father took up stations some thirty yards removed and I saw each in turn settle down on the bank.

At this precise moment in my life a further wonderful thing happened within me although I was not fully aware of the transition. I was freezing up bodily and becoming absorbed into my environment. I was still. Awake and yet motionless. Being accepted by my surroundings as part of them and no longer violating the natural pattern of nature. My eyes wandered away from the bobbing cork and steered a passage through little whirlpools of reflected sunlight to spears of rush which jutted and fanned in movement. They caught the glint of a large brown dragonfly, poised like a brooch and spreading its lattice wings to harden. Here was a bulbous beetle nudging upwards to the sky on a leafy track which narrowed with every step. And there a hairy caterpillar, coiling and arching in an opposite direction. Tiny spawn flittered in the shallows and then darted away, fast as light, should an unfamiliar movement startle them. Now came a jerking moorhen, plucking and probing, its bright eye watchful and cheeky tail never still. All around the hum of inspects and the gurgling water. A willow warbler trilled a plaintive melody, echoed by another along the stream, and a starling chattered from a corner of the stable tiles.

This was sweet unadulterated summer and time stood still. I was suddenly startled by a loud shout from Sam which shattered my daydream. He had hooked a fish and appeared to be having the greatest difficulty in preventing his capture pulling him into the brook. My father and I hurried to his assistance and we found that Sam's line was now stretched taut into a deep pool under some bushes.

"'E ent aff a big 'un!" exclaimed Sam excitedly as we came up to him. "Took me rod right under an' he's still on!"

As we stood watching, Sam's line suddenly became slack and then plunged at another angle which sent the crop straining upstream. When the fish felt the unyielding line it turned into the bank on our side round the back of a clump of rush and was momentarily still.

"Try and keep the end of the rod up," said my father. But hardly had he spoken when the fish was away again. Sam, however, quickly appreciated the importance of this manoeuvre and stopped the next sudden dash in mid-stream. As it turned I saw a thick spotted golden streak plunge deep into the dark green water and then disappear.

"It's a trout," exclaimed my father. "Don't let it get away."

Sam was able gradually to keep the fish nearer the surface and after several further futile dashes it was trailed splashing across the water and dragged out onto the bank.

To those who fish there can be no greater satisfaction than the wondrous trout. If the catching of him were not enough to stimulate the mind then indeed his very appearance must. Though ferocious in habit and cold-blooded in purpose yet has nature given him grace to kill. And kill he must with all his strength and shapely beauty. Now in his own death a thing of wonder and of colour, of pinks and golds and silver greys, painted over with the immaculate freshness of wet varnish. He lay there in the grass, the proud possession of Sam, the country boy, who had no split cane rod nor fixed spool reel.

The three of us marched triumphantly to the dairy, with Sam in the middle carrying his fish. My grandmother approvingly did the weighing on her butter-scales and the weight was established as a dram less than two pounds.

On a plate, in a mesh-fronted meat safe, the trout remained in the cool until Sam went home in the evening, while we returned happily to the brook in search of further adventure.

Away down-stream we found miller Claud White, clearing

fallen branches from his millpond and, as this appeared to be an attractive occupation, we set aside our rods to help him.

To get legitimately wet was delightful. Sam in particular took full advantage by wading about, fully clothed, with the water up to his arm-pits. His efforts were highly rewarding because he was able to fasten a rope on to several snags which had resisted hitherto. The old miller was delighted and complimented Sam who, in turn, beamed like a water-spaniel as he plunged through weed and mud.

An hour later, a number of knarled, black and sodden branches sprawled on the bank like prehistoric reptiles, stretching dead distorted limbs from the lush grass. The water, now freed from snags and flotsam, took on an appearance of stale cocoa as it moved more steadily into the old mill.

Sam resisted the suggestion that he should go home and change his clothes. I now strongly suspect that this was because his wardrobe was quite empty but the thought did not occur to me at the time. Bed for Sam was an unsatisfactory alternative. He accordingly shed all his outer garments, leaving them in the sun to dry and trooped with us into the old mill, wearing only his combinations. Some tea was brewed in a pale blue enamelled pot and we took it in turns to drink heartily from a large white cup which had no handle.

Inside the mill there was twilight and this kept us temporarily unaware of all save the large objects. But, as we sat drinking the tea, a more detailed environment grew around us and fixed itself in an everlasting memory: a photographic process of slow exposure producing infinite definition emprinted for a lifetime.

At first the shafts of sunlight which pierced the gloom had full command, holding prisoner myriad particles of silver dust before bearing bright on the flag-stone floor. Then we saw the great circular altar of stone which ground the corn, resting in its troughing, but temporarily divorced from its mate suspended a few feet above. Hoppers and bins of several sizes and shapes bore the imprint of years of constant use and they ousted grain onto the floor through numerous cracks and rat-holes. A length of rope which controlled the sack hoist stretched upwards, wearing an irregular hole in the boarded floor above and, nearby, its fellow dangled through a double flap in the ceiling and this supporting an iron hook, shining bright.

All around were shaftings and big wheels, leather belts and black gummy streakings of oil.

The miller had his rough partitioned office near the door which afforded him only sufficient room to stand before a chest-high desk. On this, several piles of papers were impaled on spikes, there were two pens, an old iron ink-stand and a freshly-killed rabbit.

When the tea-drinking was over, the miller explained to my father how the corn was brought by the farmers in their wagons and the process of grinding it into flour. But the fact which impressed me most was that old Claud White spent his working days alone. I had not thought of this possibility before and I felt a little sad. The miller may have sensed my despair because he placed a mealy hand on my shoulder and said, "Thee cum along tamorrah wen oi be grindin an lend an 'and; two ken allus do better then won."

We tarried a while longer that day to watch the chipping which was effected with meticulous care. A leather apron was taken from a hook, a chisel and mallet from a cupboard and a pair of steel rimmed spectacles from a drawer in the desk. Then the old man, gingerly kneeling on some sacking, adjusted the spectacles on the end of his nose and commenced chipping shallow grooves across the lower millstone. The chisel followed a still discernible pattern on the almost smooth surface which was patched in corduroy; each piece its own particular shape; each piece antagonistic to its fellows.

The procedure was slow and laborious. Little progress had been made when we departed. As we walked away along the lane the chipping was still ringing in our ears. Work would go on by lamp light into the night.

What better was there to do in those far-away times?

If it had no other, the Prout family possessed one qualification which afforded some claim to notoriety. It was large — very large. George, my grandfather, had succeeded in providing me with six uncles and as his own numerous brothers were equally prolific, there always seemed to be hordes of people living comparatively near to Standish who bore the family name.

It was not unreasonable, therefore, that on occasion and when the demands of agriculture permitted, the Prouts should band themselves together to form a cricket team. These functions appeared to be somewhat spasmodic and I suspect that, more often than not, cricket matches were the outcome of rash wagers accepted in local cider-cellars. Nevertheless, the family was able usually to give a good account of itself, although perhaps all the finer skills of the game were not present during the encounter.

A few months after my return to Standish and when the morning milking was done, Uncle Robert took me to a large flat meadow by the brook. I rode on the back of Duke who was harnessed to an iron roller which clanked noisily as the castings butted against each other. Duke was normally employed on much heavier draft but was well suited to this occupation because he was quiet and would carry out the task at a steady pace, which was all that was required. It was a holiday for him too and he showed his appreciation by twitching his ears and sluvvering his nostrils.

It was just an ordinary meadow where the cows had been grazing and this was amply apparent to a casual observer. There were moist and sloppy patches, swarming with golden-brown flies in nuptial animation and others, well dried, and surrounded with tufts of lush grass.

Ephraim Harris was already busy with his scythe on a small rectangle in the middle of the field but he gladly stopped his steady pendulum to drain a jar of cider which we had brought with us. Sam's father had a capacity second-to-none and he only operated at his best after the third jar. With two already consumed during milking and breakfast, he was now in prime condition.

He bent down and placed the empty drinking tot over the

cork in the jar. Then he wiped his long black whiskers on a red handkerchief which he afterwards stuffed back into a trouser pocket.

"Ther be nowt like a drop ov oil ter kip the wheels aturnin!" he said.

We waited a few minutes while Ephraim finished the cutting and then the patch was rolled steadily until dinnertime.

Back in the spacious farm kitchen where was a buzz of excitement and chatter. Some uncles and aunts were eating and drinking, while all appeared to be talking. The place-settings on the table were ignored and Uncle Martin was carving healthy portions from a baron-of-beef which he administered with dexterity to a perambulating clientele.

On a side-table, a wall of sandwiches grew steadily, but not without illicit interruption. Lemonade by the bucketful dissolved from golden crystals and gurgled into an army of bottles. Slabs of cake and hunks of bread-and-cheese were shrouded with linen into fruit baskets. All to be set upon later in the day.

Around two o'clock, I joined a cavalcade of ankle-length white skirts, lace and black stockings which wound its way through the rick-yard and along by the brook.

In the cricket meadow was assembled already at least three score of the local community and this number increased every minute as fresh arrivals clambered over gates and stiles.

Jovial and bewhiskered Canon Nash, a gaiter-black hub to a swirling feminine wheel of white satinette, shook each in turn by hand.

Two farm wagons had been drawn up, end to end, to serve as a pavilion and in them were people on benches and chairs. The whole was a scene of carnival and of cricket — real country cricket, where rules were made to be broken.

I do not remember who it was provided the equipment for the match but the umpires discovered, when they were pressed into duty, that one of the bails was missing. The bag containing the gear had remained in the farm kitchen for most of the morning and it is not unreasonable, I suppose, that suspicion should fall on the infant who had unfastened the straps. I did my best to establish my innocence but I fear that circumstantial evidence was strong.

However, the inevitable was at last accepted. The match was played with three bails and the peg from a rabbit-trap which 'Poot' Spiers conveniently found in his pocket. In fairness to the batsmen, an exchange was made when each over was completed, so that the peg was always on the wickets at the bowler's end.

When the umpires had been briefed concerning their duties and it had been agreed that a ball into the brook was a four, they went out onto the pitch with the two captains to set the wickets. But here again was further difficulty. Nobody was quite certain how far apart the wickets should be and, in any case, Willie Smart had forgotten to bring his tape measure.

"I be fer certain un be a chaane, like wat 'um de measure 'edges," said Ben Ewers. "But danged if I der know if it be frawm creese or frawm wickuts."

Ben, who wore a pair of heavy hobnailed boots beneath his long fawn milking smock, presently solved the problem himself. A heel-to-toe tight-walk, sixty-six boots long, set the distance and the stumps were pushed in. The length was further checked by one of the visiting team's bowlers who unleashed a series of very erratic balls between the wickets and, in conclusion, he pronounced the distance satisfactory.

The captains, wearing white flannel trousers, and chosen because they possessed blazers with breast-pocket badges, now tossed a coin and soon the tidings passed right round the field — "The Prouts be in fust!"

Aunt Emily accepted the heavy responsibility for keeping the score and although I could not at this time count even the fingers on one hand, I had no hesitation in electing myself as her assistant. My aunt's impartiality must have been above suspicion because both teams were prepared to rely on her accurate record. This was perhaps as well because there was only one scorebook and that provided by our visitors.

At this point the visiting captain led his men onto the field. There were eleven of them. The fact was noted with satisfaction by the spectators because it was not uncommon for country teams to try to obtain an advantage by fielding an extra player.

The Haresfield side had the stamp of authority as it strode confidently out to the wickets. At least six of its members were in white flannel trousers and only two were wearing braces. Though there was a dispersion of brown boots, there was not a black pair in the whole team.

The field was set in a professional manner as two of my uncles, Oswald and Robert, walked sedately away from one of the farm wagons. Each was in white from head to foot and each was wearing a blue peaked-cap which denoted association with the Stonehouse Club. In these two the hope lay, for indeed they were the only regular performers in the whole family side.

"Good old Bob, 'it 'um fer six!" shouted George Hughes and his outburst stimulated the onlookers, now well swollen in number, to bawl encouragement from all points of the compass.

While Oswald and Robert remained together runs came steadily. The pace was slow but it was sure and for some twenty minutes they ran up and down between the wickets at regular intervals. At the offset, every stroke was applauded, but, as time wore on, even the wags lost some of their exuberance. Nervous tensions relaxed and everyone settled down to clapping just the scoring shots.

Occasionally a ball went whizzing into the crowd, scattering young and old alike, and this called for a further outburst of enthusiasm. On one occasion Oswald hit a ball into the brook and later Robert skied one into the lane.

Things looked very rosy indeed. So much so, that George Hughes, in a further expression of family loyalty, bawled, "Thees nevir git 'um out 'aresfield, whoi done 'y giv' up!"

But the arrogance of the moment was short-lived, there was a simple snick, a loud "Howzatt!" and one of the uncles was walking towards us.

Now came Uncle Ernest. He too in white flannels. The last remaining pair in the team. When the batting pads had been exchanged — there was no surplus of luxury — Ernest went out to prevent the breakthrough.

For a while longer the family held out but Haresfield were anxious to slash the long tail and soon they were cutting it in pieces.

Uncles and cousins, both 'first-remove' and 'step', came and went and only Ernest stood his ground. He plodded along in company with an ever-changing array of boots and braces as the wickets tumbled. All appeared lost, when for last-man, a pair of breeches and brown leather leggings came in. They belonged to Uncle Percy. Those breeches and brown leggings, like the wild horses they rode, just kicked and kicked and kicked. Leather was hunted from far and wide and each fresh bowler took an increasing punishment. When the ball did not land completely out of the field, those breeches and brown leggings scampered up and down between the wickets, to a roar which was now continuous.

Twice it looked very much as though Uncle Percy had been 'run-out', but no umpire could afford to spoil this riot of fun and the appeal was rejected to the delight of the parish.

At last his wicket was shattered at a time when he was swinging his bat in the middle of the pitch so that the innings was ended in a thoroughly positive manner.

Everyone now seemed to surge towards Aunt Emily and myself to find out the final score and there were anxious moments while the complicated figures were added up.

At last my aunt stood up from her bench on the wagon and proudly announced, ''The Prouts have scored ninety-seven and a half!''

The effect was startling. The sea of upturned and expectant faces clouded and bewilderment followed where there should have been cheers. Uncle Robert jumped up onto the wagon and quickly took the scorebook to see for himself.

Then he burst out laughing.

This certainly relieved the tension whilst a rapid consultation between my aunt and uncle took place. Shortly afterwards, it was established that the Prouts had scored one hundred and fifty-one runs. Aunt Emily, with her school-day 'rounders' in mind, had thought that it was necessary for each batsman to travel up and down between the wickets before qualifying for a full run. Only the boundary shots had been registered at actual value!

In the fine spirit of the match, the Haresfield team, after much joking and prattle, accepted the target set them as valid and with the rest of us, waded into ample refreshments.

For the second time this day I ate standing up. Only this time there were many more people doing the same thing. The whole parish was eating at once and I remember thinking of the brown caterpillars on the patch of nettles at the back of the stables. What a lot of food things eat. One day everything would be eaten and then we must start eating each other. We were doing this already. I had helped to eat part of a bullock at lunchtime. The matter soon became too complicated, so I returned to the present and watched Ephraim eating. He was good at it. His hands were full of food and a large clasp knife. He had a 'chunk' of bread, a 'hunk' of cheese and a 'dab' of butter. There was also a thick slice of ham and a big onion. The bread in his left hand formed a base to the ham, the cheese and the butter, while the right hand held the knife with the onion pressed against the handle. The knife sawed things from the left hand, spread butter on them and the point conveyed the segments to Ephraim's mouth. When he wanted onion to enrich the flavour, he just gnawed it with his brown teeth. It all seemed so simple, yet I had butter and the drippings from a breakfast-egg on the front of my jersey.

Canon Nash nibbled sandwiches, one at a time. Perhaps he had never been taught to eat country-fashion and, in any case, it would be a great pity to get butter on his black satin neck-piece.

I noticed too that the party from the vicarage — and indeed some of my more sophisticated relatives — alternated between eating sandwiches and drinking tea, while the true country people concentrated on eating and left the drinking until afterwards. Much more sensible I thought.

Some ate fast and some ate slow. Some ate more than

others but all ate a lot.

When the eating was finished there was nothing left because Boyno and Spot did a thorough tour of all the baskets and licked out the bucket where all the milk had been.

Now came the drinking. Most of the cricketers had tea or lemonade and the cider barrel was left for the supporters. But George Hughes had other ideas. He reasoned that if some of the Haresfield team could be persuaded just to sample a cask made from prime fruit which he could highly recommend, then the match was 'as good as in the bag'.

Fortunately this deep-laid plot was discovered in good time by Uncle Martin and the family escutcheon when untarnished.

However, it would not have been the first time that such intrigue succeeded in a cricket match. It will by no means be the last. Suffice it to say, that, on this occasion, the encounter was continued with all participants completely sober.

The Prouts now spread themselves over the field and the Haresfield opening batsmen prepared themselves for shock tactics from cousins Grayham and Burton.

Grayham's second ball shattered the wicket at Frank Chandler's end and further success came a few overs later when John Dyke was caught in the slips. There was a brief stand which produced a dozen runs and then a collapse. A wicket fell to Burton and, in the next over, two to Grayham with consecutive balls. Half the Haresfield side was out for twenty-three runs.

The spectators were quite satisfied that the game was over and a strange sympathetic quiet permeated the field. They were not looking for a crushing defeat of either side. It was not in the nature of things for country people to rejoice in humiliation.

The incoming batsman was a short, thick-set fellow with a round, amiable and red face. His trousers were hitched up within the batting-pads so that the backs of the turn-ups stood out like a pair of rudders. His chubby fore-arms were thick with long fair hair and the back of his head was sunflower bald.

When he reached the wicket he took a quick look round and then he squared up to the next ball from Grayham. It came fast and true — and equally fast and true it landed in the millpond.

There was no effort in the stroke. Just a sudden contortion of the shoulders like the springing of a trap.

Few saw the passage of the ball and only when a party of fielders gathered at the water's edge did the belated thunder of applause echo the lightning strike.

Again and again the ball cracked to the boundary with never a false stroke and the family stumbled and collided in futile effort.

Eighty, ninety, one hundred, and Haresfield were catching up. There appeared to be no way of stopping this man. But with thirteen further runs scored his partner ran him out.

As he walked away from the wicket a few drops of rain began to fall and the sky darkened overhead. Black clouds, unnoticed in our excitement, were rolling up the Severn.

Not a moment must be lost now. A decision was vital so that debts could be paid. How else would there be satisfaction? For ten minutes more Haresfield went valiantly for the runs and the Prouts tried equally hard to take their wickets.

Though I would wish to tell otherwise there was no conclusion. A sudden downpour sent the players scurrying for shelter with one wicket standing and five more runs to get.

Chapter three
Always cider

Cider, cider, always cider, the integument of country life. Made in vast quantity every autumn and disappearing steadily, day by day, throughout the year. It flooded annually, filling again very reservoir to a point of complete saturation, then it oozed away and was relieved by countless parched and anxious gullets which could always account for more.

Cider was a necessity. It had to be close at hand and men predetermined their actions so that they did not become isolated from supply. Cider sustained and impelled, it soothed and it fortified. It gave to all the stimulus for work and for living.

If George or Ephraim, Tom or Harry went to the fields then they took cider with them and the quantity was decided by the time they would remain out of contact with the cellar.

It was no accident that the stoneware jars had wicker jackets and ring handles. How better could they hang from the curving hames? Each was essential to horse and man when work was to be done and cider was part of the team.

Late one September I watched three of my farm companions uncover a large platform which had been at the back of the wagon-shed and draw it out into the sunshine.

Through the summer months, this strange device, shrouded in sacking, had crossed many an ocean to lands of childhood imagination. As captain, I had turned the wheels and handles of the superstructure in fanciful navigation. Now it moved to perform a proper function and my daydreams were no more.

Once outside, 'the cider-maker' was thoroughly scrubbed and cleaned and the moving-parts lubricated with thick green oil taken from a flattened cocoa tin. Then it was bait-time.

The last mouthfuls of bread had scarcely been swilled down when George Hughes and Sam arrived with a team of horses and a wagon load of apples. They were followed immediately by a smaller trolley which had a huge stack of fibre matting piled on its bed.

Maurice Underwood came from the garden and Ephraim from the cow-stalls until, by ones and twos, all the menfolk had assembled. None must miss the cider-making.

If there was labour to spare then it was not apparent, for each found a useful duty to perform. Maybe a basket full of apples could be lifted single-handed but how much better it swung when there were two pairs of arms. The apple-mill had a turning-handle on either side and was two-man in design. Nevertheless, it rotated more easily if power was produced by two double sets of pistons.

"Now then me 'arties, yer's grit in yer gizzards," sang out George as he helped to propel the first basket of apples into the hopper. "Let's zee wat yeh kin do we that little lot."

The handles turned, there commenced a crunching noise, and the pale golden husk splattered out from below the mill.

Ephraim, armed with a broad-shovel polished like a fair-day frying pan, spread the husk in the press. First there was a sheet of matting, near twice the size of the frame and overlapping all round so that the centre only was evenly covered with apple-pulp. Then the ends and sides were turned over onto the husk and a further sheet inserted on top.

Soon the press was stacked with fruity mattresses and the head-plate lowered until it was tight. Strong brown arms wound the worm-gear. Again it was cider-time, the genesis of another year in the country. Her spirit flowing out into a galvanized bucket with the mellow fruitfulness of the poet Keats.

He who would patiently watch a cider-press must ensure that he selects one well removed from a wasp nest. There were always swarms of these 'Ot vooted varmints' ready to fly in for Standish cider-making. Cap-slashing, swearing and stings were all part of the ritual, but this added a humorous flavour

This one horse power portable cider press is fully loaded and ready to produce the precious juice. Its owner, the late Ernest Morgan of Longhope, stands proudly by. [Courtesy Mrs B. Pritchard]

for all, save the unfortunate.

In the country, no small boy can hope to be immune for long. If he sits near a pile of apple-husk, even for a short while, then he can expect to feel that burning jab which hurts to the point of tears. Four times I howled and four times I was un-buttoned for examination so that further sitting became almost an impossibility. The 'blue-bag' was administered liberally to my posterior but, apart from changing the colour of my skin, I felt no immediate benefit. It was little consolation to know that the now inebriated and 'trigger-happy' insects were also taking toll of the adults. My buttocks smarted and felt on fire. Only the fear that I might be considered a coward if I went indoors kept me, a miserable snivelling creature, in the place of con-tinuing danger.

I was not sorry when the final bucket of cider was carried away to the cellar and the army of helpers followed it into the cool. 'The last oozings' were left exclusively to the yellow-and-black-banded tormentors now crawling everywhere.

It was by no means my first visit to the cider-cellar and for me there were no fears. Unlike so many cobweb-infested vaults below ground, this one at Standish had a step up into it.

A cellar in name only, but in what other manner could it be described. This windowless, spacious whitewashed room, held, in season, several thousand gallons of cider, compacted in rotund wooden casks which filled the place like circus elephants.

I loved the smell in this cool chamber. Here men came and sat in sweat-damp corduroy and smoked their clay pipes in an atmosphere of blue swirling mustiness. Here were told, again and again, the stories of the countryside to the accompaniments of wooden cask taps which fluted and squeaked.

Here was the very heart of things. Here was cider.

We all sat or stood around while Uncle Robert drew off a large stoneware tankard of the new apple juice. This trickled out of a cask, freshly acquired from a Gloucester wine merchant, which would impart a subtle flavour of rum to the maturing cider. Time must elapse for this process to be completed and the cider might be fed on other ingredients during the period as fancy directed. Beef steak, brown sugar and raisins have found their way into many a cask and there were strange and secret potents talked about only in whispers.

But this would be all in good time. The purpose now was one of assessment of things to come. A small quantity only which would not purge the stomach.

A full three quarts the tankard held and by its three handles it was passed quietly around. Each, as he drank, held two handles and passing on to the next in turn, he proffered the vanact third. The tankard rotated slowly as it moved around, a solar system in miniature lighting up face after face. Only when the tankard had returned to Uncle Robert did comment come. Ephraim was the recognised authority; he must give his verdict, and few would disagree.

"Twill maake guid zider by teh time I be a'plowin' Cowleaze. Bung 'in up Jarge afore theese perishers gits too much down."

The tap was removed and a round peg inserted in its place. This was driven home with a wooden mallet until it was tight. Ephraim watched this procedure carefully and when he was satisfied that the cider would not leak, he stood up from his stool. Then his right hand described a slow circular movement over his stomach and he smiled a little ruefully. "Cum on you blokes, thurs still werk to be dun. Time fer sittin arown on yer backsides ader milkin."

With that he went out and the rest of the countrymen followed him.

There would be more cider made tomorrow.

In my small life, the next day was always a long way off. It was impossible to reach without undressing for bed, washing and the dark. As I found none of these things attractive the bridge between one day and the next was hard to contemplate without a feeling of impending gloom.

I had already found that 'grown-ups' traded on this nocturnal barrier, using it to delay indefinitely things I wanted and could not have. There was always a degree of uncertainty about tomorrow. At least I did not prepare for bed with any enthusiasm. With four wasp stings in my buttocks my temperament was decidedly peevish.

So began the night.

I usually fell asleep without effort but now the air was hot and the bedclothese were heavy. My nether-regions burned in a trough of sticky bed feathers and the hard lumps of poison under my skin throbbed and ached. My stomach had accepted more than its fair share of apple-pulp and new cider was also imprisoned there. To add to the discomfort of the night, this mass now rumbled in open revolt.

With every passing minute my plight became more desperate until at last the point of capitulation was reached and I could stand the pain no longer.

"Aunt Emily," I bawled, "I wants to go awful bad!" As a child in the country such surrender was no easy decision because it involved a sudden physical exodus from the warm to a small stone building at the top of the garden. A naked going-out into a wilderness of draught and shadow. Where things rustled, things screeched and things flew into the candle.

The oasis, when reached, provided little comfort and one

stayed no longer than necessary to satisfy abdominal requirements. Once inside, the door was brushed through a curtain of hanging ivy, and the candle spluttered to a temporary calm.

The room was functional to the point of stark austerity, having no furniture save the battery of three earth closets with a little one at the end. A simple benching of scrubbed boarding containing round holes which diminished in size from left to right with a stage down for the children. Circular discs of wood covered the holes when not in use and you sang or whistled when in occupation during the daytime as the door had no lock.

On the whitewashed walls hung a number of Prize Cards and Rosettes from the local Fat Stock Show and a tattered Auctioneer's Almanac. There was also a framed picture of a Grecian female, prostrate with grief, and clinging to a stone cross in a grey churchyard.

The pilgrimage up the garden was made on three occasions because the pinching in my stomach would not let me remain in bed. Finally, from sheer exhaustion I fell asleep.

Then came a nightmare of candle journeys through apple-mountain lands which swarmed with black-and-yellow insects and I splashed in a brook which flowed with cider.

At last, the dawn, and a morning blackbird, below my window, called me to reality.

My cider baptism was complete.

It happened one Sunday morning when the Standish bell-ringers were in the cider cellar. Indeed, it could have happened on any Sunday morning for this was the pattern of things for those who rang bells.

Canon Nash did not altogether approve but he must tolerate the situation or go bell-less, in silence, to his pulpit.

Uncle Martin had no particular interest in the ringing of Sunday bells but he was concerned for the gallons of cider which disappeared while the village knelt in prayer. It was the custom for the ropes to be pulled, both before and after the service, but the ringers had developed a preference for cider to sermons in the interim.

Uncle Martin may well have continued to suffer in silence, but a limit was reached when the St. Dunstan's Doubles were stampeded as the faithful filed from church.

A week had gone by and something must be done. Matters were going from bad to worse and so on this Sunday morning things happened.

The party from the belfry had already assembled in the cider-cellar and the three-handled tankard was having its second filling when Uncle Martin timed his easy entry.

"Be you going to 'av a swig, Gaffer?" asked Rubin James, rather condescendingly, as he drew in a hobnailed boot and tucked it under his seat, "We 'ant drunk you out of 'ouse an' 'ome yet an' we'm glad te 'av th' oppertunity ov yore company. 'Tis darn gud zider!"

Uncle Martin took a long pull at the tankard and then handed it back.

Rubin waited for him to finish and then continued rather apprehensively, "Us bin 'earin the Canon wer a bit upset 'bout las' wick. Quite thawt you wood 'a stopped tap on us, but tawld 'un, no cider, no bells, an' we 'ant bin let down."

The bell-ringers agreed to a man that everyone was being most reasonable and the tankard was refilled and passed round again.

Uncle Martin waited his time and only when all nervousness had departed did he have anything to say. Then he told the men in a most pleasant manner that he would always be glad for them to have the freedom of the cellar on Sunday mornings. In future, however, it might be as well for them to stick to one cask and not to mix their drinks. No doubt that was how the damage had been done. Some of his special casks were pretty strong. He would in future put a chalk cross on the cask to be used and then there would be no risk of further trouble.

The bell-ringers glanced at each other as they nodded approval and they had great difficulty in concealing the relief they all felt. In spite of earlier fears, they could in future have as much cider as they wanted. No problem at all to draw it from the marked cask.

The atmosphere, which was strained at the commencement, now became mellowed with ciderly influence. The tankard continued its circumnavigation from port to port, shedding its cargo liberally as it went.

Five or six more times it went round before Uncle Martin announced, "I'd best be getting round the young cattle. Folks will soon be out of church and t'will be dinner time else."

As he stood up, he drove a hand deep into the pocket of his smock and then, with just the right amount of fumbling to attract complete attention, he drew out a full-grown dead rat. The animal was carefully combed and stroked by Uncle Martin's fingers to remove sundry bits of chaff and a whisp of soft string. It was held by the tail while the bung was removed from the top of a large cask and then it disappeared head-first through the hole. Before the bung was replaced, and for good measure, a second rat was patiently groomed and committed with due ceremony in the same manner.

Not a word was spoken while Uncle Martin wiped his fingers in a handkerchief and his bright 'Cheerio' went almost unanswered as he disappeared through the door.

"Well Oi be danged!" said Patrick Meek, breaking the stunning silence. "Oude a'thart 'e 'a dun that? 'Ave 'urd tell of ded rats afore but now Oi sid it we me own eyes! No wonder 'ees zider gits strawn, fed on vermin. Shan't be keen t'drink none owt a thick carsk."

"Wot abowt th'won we bin a'guzzelin then?" volunteered Rubin James, bringing the awful truth home to his companions. "Ye ken bet thame awl treeted aloike."

"No wonder we all got 'up-the-pole' larst wick," added Simon Tranter by way of explanation. "The tenor bell were bangin in me 'ed all adernoon. Oi new summat wer up. Zider nevir dun that to Oi befowr."

A rather bewildered party returned later to the belfry where it rang the final peal with no great enthusiasm. Then it dispersed in a state of apprehension without knowing quite what to expect from the future.

During the days that followed, tongues wagged and heads

nodded and soon the whole parish knew one side of the story. But it was too hot a chestnut to be swallowed in a large lump and there were those with misgivings.

Martin Prout, it was argued, did not put dead rats in his cider and for certain it was an empty cask. The rats were without doubt removed later. It was just a prank.

But the master-mind remained silent and with cool determination played out his hand. The chalk cross was on the fateful cask when the bell-ringers assembled the following Sunday.

"Oi'l dare thee, Jarge!" said Rubin, as he sat himself down on an upturned bucket. "Tap 'im an zee wot cums owt."

The tap was turned and there trickled down a fluid as dark as vinegar which appeared to have little lumps in it. George Parson's big red nose followed the liquid into the tankard, sniffing like a ferret, and then was withdrawn by its owner who gasped, "It stinks loike 'ell in the nite. Oi ent drinkin none ov thaat."

This was complete stalemate. The bell-ringers knew that, short of taking matters into their own hands, they would go thirsty back to the belfry. Cider there was, everywhere, but never a drop to drink. It was indeed a cruel world and for several minutes it remained that way.

But the angel of mercy now entered to save the situation. With a wry smile, Uncle Martin chuckled, "I thought perhaps you gentlemen might find the cask I marked a bit strong so I've drawn off a couple of jars of sweeter stuff for them who like their cider undoctored. You'll find the jars in the corner."

And here the matter ended.

For ever afterwards, Uncle Martin put out two jars of cider for the bell-ringers on Sunday mornings but he kept his secret to himself.

To this very day, no one really knows the full story of the rats in the cider cask; if they do — 'they 'ent tellin.'

Chapter four
Christmas cousins

I first noticed the autumn because of the candles at teatime. The Virginia creeper outside my bedroom window was splattered blood red and its leaves piled against the garden wall.

"Nights be a'drawin in," I was told by Maurice Underwood. "We'm goin ter 'ave an 'ard winter this yer Oi d'recon. Ye best git yer Aunt Emily te knit ee a pair of mittens, thees 'il want 'em afore long."

And so the days became colder and shorter. My ears tingled and I was provided with a blue overcoat with brass sailor buttons down the front.

One morning a large flock of starlings descended on the yellowing elder thicket and devoured all the glossy black berries. When they had gone, their purple droppings were everywhere and the little trees quite bare. Rude, noisy birds with no thought for tomorrow. Yet so cheerful as they chattered and screamed.

I ran round the thicket shouting at them but they paid little heed. The nearest hundred would rise momentarily and then jettison themselves in a more convenient place just twenty yards further away.

It was Sam who discovered the best method. He banged some corrugated iron with a big stick and there was a sudden silence. The startled mass rose into the air, a heavy wheeling cloud; but like water from a bucket, it poured itself back into the thicket and the tumult grew again.

The birds would not be driven away until all was devoured. Young humans must not interfere with the process of nature.

Her cruel purpose must follow in the fatal berry-less days now not far away.

At sometime in November, when the air was damp and a soft mist hung along the stream, there came suddenly a scarlet memory. Dogs and horses were there and a copper horn which purped.

For a long time I remained with my nose pushed hard against the kitchen window. But, at last, I crept unnoticed to the stone step by the dairy door where I had a better view. I would have remained unobtrusive had not a large hound washed my face with its pink, sloppy tongue. Quite suddenly, I had become a part of the doggy throng and I was moving more into the centre of things.

All went extremely well until another hound, lurking behind, hung its front half over my shoulders and I fell flat on my face. In a moment the pack was all around and a mass of waving tails closed in on me. Paws, bellies and sluggy noses provided a canine envelopment and I could not rise from the ground.

I was rescued by a huntsman whose sharp command caused a hole to open up above me. Here I sat in complete bewilderment, watched by a circle of enquiring brown eyes, sloping in pairs, as each upper ear cocked cheekily. Beyond there were laughing human faces. As quickly as possible, I escaped back to the kitchen.

My understanding grandmother led me to an attic window where I could better witness the departing Hunt. It soon passed out through the stone archway at the end of the drive and was followed by many Standish folk on foot. When it had gone, I could not help remarking to my grandmother that I thought it was an awful lot of fuss just to catch a little fox. Why did they have to wear those red coats and why did they need so many dogs and people?

I was not entirely satisfied with the explanations I was given but grandmother let something slip out which caused me much concern. Small boys and sometimes girls were 'blooded', so it appeared, and this was done by smearing the face with the dead fox's brush, after it had been cut off. Having considered this, I was perfectly satisfied that Uncle Martin would do me when he returned home and the thought was in no way appealing. There was no alternative, therefore, but to spend several hours in hiding in a thick laurel bush in the garden from whence I did not reappear until long after my bedtime.

Blooding I did not get, but I did get a whale of a ticking off. It was indeed a very scarlet memory!

And now it was Christmas. For at least a month the preparations had been going along. As far as had been permitted by my elders, I had contrived that my grubby hands should become involved in the many Yuletide labours. Perhaps my efforts were not always appreciated but at least my intentions were good even though mistakes were made. Clean hands were ordered for pudding-mixing, although I was allowed but a token stir as a final gesture. My main forte had been a liberal tasting of the ingredients and the insertion of numerous small silver threepenny pieces into the mixture. There was, of course, a slight accident when an egg had somehow become broken on the hearth rug but the dog had licked up most of it and, fortunately, the incident had passed unnoticed. If the truth were known, I was better at fetching and bringing than at mixing and fixing, but I did my best.

Mistletoe had been clipped from some tall old fruit trees growing at the top of the big orchard, holly had been cut from the thicket beyond Court Hill and a large Yule log had been carefully selected from the stack of firewood heaped behind the stables. More recently, we had driven the turkeys to a small shed at the back of the dairy — unhappily for them, their last journey on foot.

A little snow had fallen earlier in the month but had melted away in a few hours. Now, on Christmas Eve, it was snowing again and the ground was hard with frost.

Ephraim, with an old sack over his head, came across the courtyard to the dairy. He had a yoke over his shoulders to which was suspended by chains a pair of milk buckets. The frothy liquid steamed in the frosty evening air as he pushed his bulk sideways through the door. Then he stooped forward, the buckets grated the wet stone slabbing and the handles fell with a clatter. Before he straightened himself he poked a horny, twisted finger playfully into my belly and, at the same time, he made a strange noise rather like a hoarse duck. This caused the old man much amusement and he laughed as he lifted each bucket high, tipping its contents into a tank bracketed to the whitewashed wall. He was still chuckling to himself when he turned a little tap which allowed the milk to trickle through a strainer and over a corrugated plate into the churn.

"I'll bet you've a mind ter pop them brass buttons off afore lawng. Admiral Jellicoe 'ill be a'struttin around with 'ees kote undun fer shure. Yer gran'ma's cookin 'il zee ter that." Then he winked at my grandmother and, with a changed voice, he said, "Will'ee tell the gaffer I've giv Buttercup an' the spotted 'effer sum linseed kake loike'ee wanted."

Ephraim then went back out into the swirling snow and was lost, save for his crunching boots, in a pale yellow gloom that was this Christmas evening.

I returned with grandmother to the great farm kitchen. A bright fire sparkled in the shining black range which had large ovens on either side. The spacious central table was set for supper on a white linen cloth with a plate and knife for each person. The centre piece to the table was a massive piece of cheese.

My sailor coat had scarcely been removed when we heard the 'clopper' of a pony and trap outside and the Parkend People had arrived. Uncle Oswald, Aunt Edith and my three cousins, Ronnie, Basil and Eileen were just the beginning. Within the hour, George Hughes had made two trips to Haresfield station and there were more ponies and traps. By suppertime the Malswick People had joined the Oakey People and the Elmore People were busily talking to the Haresfield People.

The large room was full of Prouts, their wives and their husbands and, excluding all else, I was in the company of four male cousins who were round, pink and open-eyed.

At first we felt a little shy, but soon becoming boisterous, we raced noisily through the parties of grown-ups. We bumped their elbows and spilt their drinks, we upset a card-table and spoilt an uncle's nap-hand and one of us even fell into the 'bran-tub' being prepared by Aunt Emily.

At last, patiences being exhausted, we were packed off to bed with not too much ceremony. However, we were allowed a brief period in which to hang our expectant stockings from the back of the old settle near the kitchen range. This piece of furniture, with high curving back of matched pine boarding, formed a partition against the door to the garden.

What better depository for those Christmas parcels which should have matured by morning?

The small party of errant young males was marshalled through the great hall, our nailed boots crunching the flag-stone floor. In single file now, we ascended the wide Tudor staircase with Aunt Emily's firm instruction to "Be quiet" echoing from the shadows produced by her flickering candle. Temporarily, we were mirrored in the plate-glass front of a case of stuffed birds which reached from floor to ceiling, our faces made pallid by the yellow light. The bright bead-eyes of those inert creatures staring in scornful reproach as we passed.

On the first-floor landing we were separated to go our various ways to bed. Cousin Stanley was directed to share my well-accustomed room.

"Now, no messing about you two. Get undressed quickly and get into bed. I'll be back to see you properly tucked in," said Aunt Emily, as she disappeared with the remaining cousins to other parts of the large house.

Stanley and I did as we were told. We were between the sheets when Aunt Emily returned to us.

Having ensured that all was in proper order she departed for a second time, taking away the candle and a box of matches with her. It would not do to allow such items to remain in the charge of two small boys during the night. The room darkened as the candle glided away and for a while all was silent. Then my cousin spoke. It was as if the pause was deliberate and accommodated careful consideration.

"I bags we're fust up in th'mornin te zee wot we've got fer Christmas," he said. Yes indeed, the idea was attractive. We would, most certainly, be fust up!

"But how can we be certain to wake up?" I asked.

"Easy," said Stanley. "Don't go te sleep!"

"Whot, stay awake all night?" I asked.

"Yeh, why not, it's easy," said Stanley. "We can just kip tawkin ter each other."

And so it was agreed and the verbose vigil began.

It seemed an age before a door opened somewhere below and one of our elders came up the staircase, rather unsteadily, I thought. Ten minutes later there were two more, talking in whispers, who passed our bedroom door.

"Haven't seen him since Mary's wedding, but gosh he's got fat," said a female voice which soon became a mumble and was then obliterated by the closing of a door.

Gradually, the large Prout family, becoming overcome with tiredness, separated itself into its component parts, room by room, and ultimately all was still.

My cousin and I remained awake although, one after another, our relatives fell asleep. It was no easy matter and there were several occasions when, had it not been for Stanley's enthusiasm, I am certain I must have passed into oblivion. However, I was prodded with an elbow and we went on talking.

"Wonder what the time is?" said Stanley, "Think us better go down now and not wait 'till mornin?"

After careful reflection this appeared to be the right thing to do, but of course we had not previously taken into account the problems which such a decision would bring and we were still rather inclined to ignore the fact that neither of us was capable of seeing in the dark!

Uppermost in our minds was the thought that a stack of crisp paper parcels was reclining on the old settle downstairs. We must get there at all cost.

And so two small bodies, clad in flannelette nightshirts, slipped out of the mahogany four-poster bed, one from each side. Automatically, because there was a mutual need that courage should be maintained, the small bodies lost no time in coming together.

At the bedroom door we paused a while, perhaps a little uncertain of how to proceed, our bare feet becoming acutely aware of an icy draught which gusted below the ill-fitting timber. Barely sufficient light emerged from the lace-curtained window to outline the heavy brass rim lock on the solid oak door.

Stanley turned the handle. The door creaked as it swung in towards us and apprehensively we moved out into the upper hall. If there had been any sense of security for us while in our bedroom, this was immediately lost in the Tudor environment which extended to the head of the staircase.

While nothing was said as we edged our way carefully forward I know that my cousin was experiencing difficulty in remaining brave. My own courage hinged on his capacity to lead us on. Had Stanley not stood firm when a cat suddenly dropped from a window seat I know I would have bolted.

Now we were on the top step of the stairs and below us was a well of blackness. Not even the shape of things could be seen down in this inky shaft.

It was Stanley who once again took the first step and obediently I followed him, although, by now, I would have gladly returned to our bedroom.

A grandfather clock stood in the corner of the half-landing below us. A faint glint of light reflected from the brass pendulum as it moved behind a little leaded window. A steady 'tick-tock' in perfect harmony gave us some assurance. But this was short-lived as we went on down the lower flight of stairs which discharged us into the great hall. Once again we were standing in front of the case of stuffed birds. If previously those bright bead eyes had looked scornfully at us, now they peered menacingly with evil intent.

A figure clad in rusty chain-mail and brandishing a fearsome axe dwarfed us. As did the massive head of a buffalo-looking creature which projected from an oaken shield fixed just below the ceiling. These ghoulish things, hoarded by our ancestors, and now bathed in a misty half-light were making their sinister contribution to our discomfort.

But Stanley was like steel as he turned into the passage which led to the kitchen. I followed him again into complete darkness. The kitchen door was closed and together we stood in front of it, our fingers groping for a handle.

Suddenly, a horrible sensation ran down my spine when my left hand came to rest on a coarse hairy object which had little hard ears on either side. My nervous fingers explored a partly open mouth containing rows of jagged and pointed teeth.

I could stand no more. I shrieked and bolted back to the staircase. My outcry of terror had its immediate impact on Stanley who, being unaware of the actual cause of my panic, made all haste to retreat from the undetermined danger which had so suddenly beset me.

The retreat to our bedroom was by no means well ordered. It was therefore not in the least surprising that several grown-ups with candles appeared to see what all the sudden noise was about.

"What on earth's going on then?" asked Uncle Robert, who intercepted us at our bedroom door. "You shouldn't be stampedin' around the house at this time in the mornin. Now what av you young varmints bin up to?"

"There's a wild animal loose down in the hall," I blurted, "an' it's got rough hair, an' teeth, an', an' . . ."

Without more ado, Uncle Robert glanced at Uncle Oswald, now standing beside him. "We'd better 'av a look," he said.

Uncle Oswald nodded and the two men, each holding his candle high, descended the staircase. Stanley and I followed in silence. In no time at all we reached the place of my capitulation and there, standing erect as the taxidermist had devised, was a stuffed badger, its lifeless two front paws crucified to a circle of metal rod which was the top half of an umbrella stand.

A few minutes later and we were back in bed.

"I'm awful sorry I let you down, Stanley," I said.

"Don't worry," said Stanley, mindful of the shame I had suffered. "Who ever heard tell of a badger holdin' umbrellas, just stupid!"

And we both fell asleep.

It was Monday morning and early too, because country people did not stay long in bed after it had become light, even in summertime. There were occasions when I was allowed to remain in bed after work had begun, but generally I arose with the grown-ups so that I did not miss anything.

Today was such an occasion because we were making cheese at Standish, Single Gloucester Cheese, stuff of which the family was very proud. Making cheese at Standish was not an unusual happening because vast quantities were produced every year. But every Monday saw the beginning of a new cycle as little work was done in the dairy on Sunday.

In saying 'we were making cheese', of course I meant that my grandmother was making cheese and I was getting in the way and bombarding her with questions. Nevertheless, my grandmother always appeared happy to have me in her dairy in spite of the delays I sometimes caused.

Now, today, it was all beginning again. Cheese, one of the staple productions of Standish was being made.

A massive circular vat was in the middle of the dairy. Sheets of metal riveted together and reinforced with polished brass strip formed this huge tank which stood above the flag-stone floor on a formwork of quartered oak. All shining and spotlessly clean from the periodic scrubbing which my grandmother administered every time it became empty.

Now it was full of milk, gallons and gallons of full-cream milk, to which had been added rennet.

At the appropriate time and as the curds began to form, my grandmother moved steadily around the vat, armed with a long-handled fork which had blades of steel both horizontal and vertical. This she used in the breaking-up process until there were countless hundreds of baby cubes of curd floating on the whey from which they had now separated.

When my grandmother was satisfied that the process was complete — and she alone by experience could tell — a large brass tap was turned in the bottom of the vat so that the whey could be drawn off into buckets providing food for calf and pig.

At the appropriate time and when the whey had completely drained from the curds, the massive cheese-press was brought into use. Grandmother carefully lined each wooden mould with 'cheese cloth' before filling it to overflowing with curds. The moulds were stacked one upon another in the cheese-press and the powerful capstan was wound down upon them.

Now time and the maturing process would produce the stuff for which Standish was famous, but grandmother still had much to do before the cheese would be fit for the table.

In the big cheese-room on the first floor above the dairy was the accumulation of weeks of work. Tiers of oaken shelves many yards long groaned with the weight of cheeses stacked upon them. Here my grandmother kept an almost continuous watch over the maturing process, turning the cheeses as necessary. While thus engaged, there was always close at hand a small tool which was unique. It was formed from a hollow cylinder of metal as long as a pencil which was sharpened at the open end. This was pushed down into the selected cheese and when withdrawn it contained a core of the tasty substance. A small metal plunger, when brought into use, expelled the core for examination. If it was though desirable, my grand-mother would break off a small portion of the core farthest removed from the rind and taste it before pushing the larger part back into the cheese. Thus, she was able to know how many cheeses she had ready for sale.

From time to time my grandmother was visited at Standish by Mr Aldridge from a large firm of grocers in Gloucester. Generally, a few days after this visit, a large wagon drawn by two horses and carefully stacked with cheeses left for the city. Occasionally, cheeses were sent to Haresfield station for delivery to other parts of the country and once, I was told, a cheese was sent to Holland!

If any proof was needed that Gloucester cheese was edible in large quantities then it surely was established by Uncle Oswald. He it was who often said, "A cheese is good if you can eat a pund on't without bread." On several occasions I saw my uncle prove this to his own complete satisfaction!

The flag-stone floor in the kitchen had a great attraction for me in that it provided the foundation for my developing imagination. There was no doubt whatever in my juvenile mind that someday I would become a farmer. Here below me were fields of all different shapes and sizes. All I needed now were the animals to put into them and, with the help of Aunt Emily, my farm soon became well stocked.

I had a large flock of at least fifty dried peas. The fact that the peas had no legs did not in the least upset my decision that they were Cotswold sheep. Thirty odd large black-and-mauve kidney beans were my herd of Gloucestershire milking cows and the dozen or more chestnuts were my cart-horses for sure. I had wheat Rhode Island Reds and barley Light Sussex poultry. I had hazelnut Wessex Saddle Backs and Indian corn Glo'ster Spots. The sheds and barns were cardboard boxes of various sizes and the poultry houses Moreland's 'England's Glory' boxes with the matches removed.

For long periods of the day my bare knees accepted the comfortless flag-stones as I moved my stock from field to field. I was thus absorbed, driving the flock of dried peas from a field near the sideboard to fresh pasture at the back door, when I found a pair of highly polished black boots and spurs blocking the route.

It seemed that Uncle Percy had been watching for some moments because his large frame began to shake with amusement.

"Be e' zertin the've et all the grass," he said. "Bist goin ter plow wer they cum from? Bet thees'ill find grownd a bit 'ard and stoney," he chuckled.

But the comments did not easily register with me because, as I looked up at Uncle Percy towering above, he was different, very different.

There were long narrow blue trousers with wide braid down the side of each leg, a close-fitting short blue jacket which had a 'bird-cage' of braid diminishing down the front, and up on uncle's head was a round black hairy hat.

For Uncle, in his spare time, was an officer in the Yeomanry. And now was uncle's bushy moustache fully resplendent and indeed reminiscent of the Kaiser himself.

Uncle bent down and helped me up and then he said, "Let's get yer best bib an' tucker on, 'cause we'm goin ter Stonehouse fer parade."

As if all had been previously arranged, Aunt Emily now came into the kitchen carrying my 'going-out' clothes and in these vestments I was suitably attired. In keeping with Uncle Percy, I had a navy jacket and this had four brass buttons on the front.

When we got out to the pony and trap I found that George Hughes and Bill Buckle were both waiting for us and that they were both adorned in blue uniforms. I was hoisted up without ceremony, three parts covered with an old rug and then told to "Hold tight!"

The sprightly pony was soon trotting briskly through the stone archway, past the school-house and up onto the Stonehouse road. We passed George Hughes' cottage on the left before crossing the railway bridge. Down the line a goods train was chuntering towards Gloucester.

In what seemed to be no time at all the now steaming pony came to a halt in a yard outside the hall where the parade was to be held. Here were many more sleek blue uniformed men talking and laughing. Willing hands quickly separated pony from trap and the dutiful animal was led away to a conveniently positioned stable.

Then we all trooped into the hall, now dimly illuminated by half-a-dozen large oil lamps hanging by chains from the rafters.

It was indeed a very large room and away at the far end a party of men were congregated who had brightly coloured drums and shining brass bugles. They were formed into regular lines and then by command a terrific noise was born which almost split my ears. My immediate reaction was to run away from this sudden blare of the bugles and thunder from the drums, magnified ten-fold by the confined space. But rather nervously, I held my ground.

After a while, I became accustomed to the holocaust and the rhythm-beat of the drums began to take command of my small body. I could not resist the desire to move in time with the regular percussions and I soon found myself strutting up and down in front of a dozen other spectators who sat in chairs at the side of the room.

As my confidence returned, so did I seek to become more involved. Ultimately, I was at the head of a column of troopers and then thoroughly mixed up in the ranks. A roar of laughter broke out as the parade came to a standstill and I was led firmly by the arms back to a chair.

"'m be a regermental maskot," said one. "Cocky little perisher," said another.

But the sergeant in charge was perhaps the least entertained by my spontaneous performance. His massive frame marched briskly in my direction, halted three paces from the group of chairs and then the order rang out to all and sundry: "Fer Gawd's sake kip 'im under control else 'im 'ill get 'urted!"

Then he turned right about and shouted to his men, "Get fell in!"

And fell in they got.

They were a fine body of men, albeit of varying size, but all were thick-set and solid. Smiles still flickered on their sun-tanned faces as they stood rigidly to attention.

Then the order rang out: "Draw swords!"

Glinting cold steel flashed in somewhat irregular fashion.

The sergeant was now most displeased because he bellowed at his men: "Wen I de zay draw, don't e draw, but wen I de zay draw swrods, whip 'em out smart an' mind e don't cut e self!"

The ride back to Standish in the flickering light of the two trap lamps was not without incident because ample refreshment had been taken after the parade was over. Bill Buckle

54

exchanged his hat for a small galvanised bucket. He insisted that he should salute everything he considered worthy of his attention. He shouted, "Good nite Lloyd George" as we passed a horse with its head over a gate and, "Gawd bless yer Majesty!" as we trundled by a red pillar box.

Thus were the 'yeomantry' made ready for the Kaiser's War and we all know how well the Hussars of Gloucestershire performed when put to the test.

Chapter five
Harvest Festival

A grey stone building of two floors stood, with its back to the churchyard, close to the entrance to Standish Court. Here the children of the parish and even those from further afield, were taught the 'Three R's' — Readin', Writin' and Arithmutic. These wide-eyed children came to school at a fairly early age, indeed, as soon as the mothers were satisfied that their offspring could walk safely from their homes. More often than not, the starting age was determined by the distance between home and school and was also influenced by the availability of an older child who could act as shepherd.

The leaving age was determined to a large extent by physical development. As soon as a child was big enough to work — and there was normally plenty of jobs available even though the pay was small — then schooling came to an abrupt end.

Attendance too was not consistent. Seasonal work such as poultry picking and the fruit harvest took priority over lessons. It was not surprising, therefore, that many country-folk could neither read nor write.

Two of my boy cousins came to Standish for their lessons and they walked a good two miles each way from Parkend Lodge Farm at Moreton Valence.

Ronnie and Basil Prout spent a fair period daily getting their education, but this did not excuse them, as soon as they were old enough, from giving a hand with the milking at the farm both night and morning. In settled weather and for most of the summertime, the journey to Standish was made across the fields, but for a large part of the year it was a trudge along two lanes and part of the Gloucester to Bristol road.

Of course, there was always the chance of a lift in a pony-trap or on a farm wagon, but in any event, riding or walking, there was little shelter from the rain.

The two boys joined the family at Standish Court for a mid-day meal and they normally gave a good account of themselves where Aunt Emily's cooking was concerned.

"Anyone would think they gave you nothin' to eat down at Parkend," said my aunt on numerous occasions, but the remark had little effect on my two cousins who continued to eat like a pair of caterpillars.

"I'll finish the juist in the bottom ov th' dish an' put on a bit more custard," requested Basil as a hearty meal reached its conclusion; and when the boys got up from the table, little that was edible remained on their plates.

Lesson books were far from plentiful at Standish although each cousin carried a canvas school-satchel. These were presents from an aunt and they served purpose to carry an array of trophies, the envy of their school-fellows. Each had a tin of marbles, a bag of 'conkers' and a well-chipped enamel drinking mug. Both had home-made catapults and a supply of small pebbles for ammunition. Ronnie had a battered copper hunting-horn which he kept carefully wrapped in a piece of old flannelette, and Basil a galvanized mole-trap which had a broken spring.

Merchants they were, bartering their wares whenever the opportunity for a bargain occurred. Embryo farmers taking their first subtle steps in commerce.

Comings and goings in the school were regulated by a large hand-bell excessively shaken by one of the pupils on the command of Mr Jenner, the male teacher. A clarion which terminated the turmoil of young voices at play and allowed the raucous rooks in the elms above, once again, to have their say.

When lessons were over, little time was lost in exodus. Evaporation took place in three main directions and soon my cousins were disappearing into the shadows of the overhanging hazels which skirted the lane to Moreton Valence.

Headmaster Edward Jenner stands with his primary school pupils outside the schoolhouse circa 1920. [Courtesy Tom Davis]

One fine, sunny morning, soon after the milking was done, George Hughes helped me up into a large wagon which already contained a number of the Standish folk. There were Sam and Emphraim Harris and Maurice Underwood, Bill Buckle, Uncle Robert, Spot, Boyno and Charlie Thomas.

"Mind an' not step on an' 'ay-vork," said George Hughes, carefully avoiding these implements scattered haphazard in the bed of the wagon.

In a moment I was perched in safety on an upturned cider cask and, once again, we trundled down the drive and through the massive stone archway.

Fore and aft, the wagon had been supplied with hay-ladders which rattled and swayed above me, a massive trellis of stout pink timber. Barely did the ladders miss the stonework as the wagon lurched beneath the ecclesiastic ruin.

It was but a short journey to the hayfield because it skirted the Stonehouse road, opposite the school-house and it a gateway to the lane. The five stout gate rails, green with lichen, were wrenched round against the hawthorn hedge which was well impregnated with hay captured from previous loaded wagons.

58

As we passed through, the heavy clatter dulled as the wheels ground into the soft brown earth. Only the click-click of the horse's shoes advised out continuing progress.

Far away in the middle of the large field, a party in shirt sleeves was already at work. Good progress had obviously been made because Tom Tranter was standing atop a wagon which was three-parts filled with hay.

Immediately on our arrival, Sam was directed to lead a trace-horse which was being connected in front of Duke already pulling in the shafts and I was told, "Keep clear and don't meddle."

When all was in order, an "Auld tight" rang out. Tom Tranter drove his hay-fork into the load at an angle and spread his legs to form a tripod and the wagon lurched forward to the proximity of further hay-cocks on either side. In turn, these were impaled by the curving double spikes and strong brown arms hoisted the hay aloft to Tom who secured it on his load.

A little further away, three of the village womenfolk, in long smocks, were busy with hand rakes and at the far end of the field a horse rake was being driven, up and down, by Charlie Barnes.

It was quite obvious that no contribution was expected from me, so I filled in my time by chasing brown butterflies and diving head-first into the heaps of hay. When quite exhausted, I lay on my back and allowed the warm sun to shine down on my half-naked body. Overhead wisps of white cloud were moving across a sky of azure blue and a kestrel winnowed like a spider on a gossamer as it hunted for mice now being exposed to its view.

Only the insects which occasionally settled on my bare skin prevented complete tranquillity, but ultimately, in spite of this disturbance, I fell asleep.

For an hour or more the work went on without my surveillance and when I awoke, large spots of rain were falling all around. As I rose to my feet I heard the distant rumble of thunder and I saw that the hay-makers were gathering their coats and looking for shelter. Ephraim grabbed my arm and I

Harvesting with horse and binder during the First World War.
[Courtesy Mrs C. Davenport]

was hustled with little ceremony some forty yards to a very large dead oak tree standing solitary and now silhouetted against a very angry sky. The tree was hollow and I was pushed through a hole in its side and followed by Ephraim. Bill Buckle was already sitting in a corner of the cavity and shortly afterwards Charlie Barnes came in with one of the dogs.

"This be better 'en under a waggin," said Ephraim as we made ourselves as comfortable as possible.

Looking around now in the half-light at the grey-black wooden interior, I began to appreciate the wisdom of the old man's comment. Indeed, we were in the dry, although by this time an absolute deluge was falling outside. We suffered only an occasional spot of rain which made its way down a crooked chimney from a hole in a branch about twenty feet above. The brown granulated earth on the floor was well admixed with dry rabbit pellets and there were several holes in the corners where the bunnies went below.

In a small cavity above my head were the projecting sticks of a jackdaw nest but I was assured by Charlie, "ther yun't any eggs at this time ov th' yer."

Outside the conditions became more and more violent. The sky shaded black and fork-lightning jagged its tortuous spears all around.

"Dos't thee think we'm goin t' git hit?" asked Bill Buckle of Ephraim, half nervously.

The old man did not answer immediately but after a pause he pronounced, "Lightnin' don't ever strike th' zame place twice."

And then, following further reflection he added, "Wen this tree were 'it, about ten yers back, it killed won ov th' gaffer's cows!"

It was nearly my bedtime and I was already in my night-shirt. Undressing had taken place in front of the kitchen range and I was listening to my nightly quota of 'Just William' read to me by Aunt Emily who appeared to obtain much satisfaction from the exercise. Suddenly, there was a scraping noise at the back door.

"I'll bet I know who that is," said Aunt Emily, as she rose to her feet, placing the book on the table.

I presumed that Aunt Emily's conjecture was correct because she showed little surprise when she opened the door.

All she said was, "Oh Spot, you dirty scamp!"

A wet and muddy fox terrier, with a drooping and dejected tail, slunk into the kitchen, leaving a conspicuous trail of earthy moisture across the floor to the bright fire in the range. At this point he turned towards us and, with lowering eyes, he shivered a little.

"Say a minute," said my aunt, "I'll get an old towel an' rub thee down."

Spot was then subjected to a fierce rubbing which he appeared to accept without much relish, perhaps believing that his reception was reasonably complimentary under all circumstances.

"I suppose you've bin at them badgers again you old tyrant," said his mistress. And Spot accepted that this was true by looking up at her with his brown eyes before rolling over onto his back. A few minutes later he was on his feet again when the old towel was deposited in a bucket in the scullery.

On one side of his head and covering his left eye was a black patch from which he obtained his name, and his otherwise white body was now stained the colour of milky cocoa. In this condition he was allowed to remain on the hearthrug where Spot commenced the detailed cleaning of his paws.

Spot was a happy soul and badgers formed an important part of his life. It may well be that sometime he had been professionally introduced to 'brock' but there were now many occasions when Spot, maybe through boredom or lust for adventure, went alone to the Dingle, where he disappeared below ground. Here, in the steep sides of the little valley, lived a family of badgers and who was to say whether love or hate provoked such visits by a little terrier dog?

Boyno, of course, did not engage in underground excursions. He was not built that way, for he was a sleek red setter. When Boyno needed adventure he obtained this by chasing either rabbit or hare. Normally he preferred company when thus engaged and no doubt was happiest to hunt with Uncle Robert and his gun.

On the other hand, Boyno had a working arrangement with Spot when, like a pair of magpies scouring a hedge, the two dogs acted their self-appointed roles.

It was Spot who probed the innermost tangles of vegetation while Boyno pranced around in anticipation. When the rabbit bolted, Boyno gave hot pursuit but normally the quarry swerved its way to safety in the nick of time.

Spot and Boyno were life-long companions and never was there a time when a growl disturbed a tranquil relationship. Although provided with separate plates at meal times, there was little poaching, and when this did take place, it was by common consent that one dog had eaten his fill and there were scraps for the other to finish.

Human affection was shared. If one dog was patted then the other came forward to receive similar patronage. It was quite normal for one human hand to stroke a high head while the other operated a little nearer the floor.

My every day was started by my canine friends who came thundering into my room at a fairly early hour with a much amused Aunt Emily. Normally, I was able to duck my head under the bedclothes before Boyno leapt onto the four-poster. Spot gyrated around barking loudly until he too was lifted onto the bed by my aunt to take his part in the awakening ceremony. For several minutes I contrived to prevent the dogs making personal contact by holding down the sheets tight to the bed but ultimately, following playful growls and much barking, a wet nose would find its way into my retreat and much licking and tail-wagging would ensue.

I am glad now that it was my own departure from Standish which ultimately severed my contact with Spot and Boyno, for my boyhood love for my doggy friends would have been rudely shattered had ill befallen either while I shared their lives.

My mother and her two sisters had talked the whole thing over and they were agreed. It was to be a splendid Harvest Festival. With or without the agreement of Canon Nash, they had formed themselves into an Action Committee to ensure complete success.

As many members as possible of the large Prout family must come. There would be the usual service at the church, of course, augmented with sundry innovations, and afterwards, there would be a reception at the Court. Mother and Aunt Emily would pay special attention to providing the meal while Aunt Annie would devote her attention to matters religious.

My aunt was no stranger to Standish Church for in her maiden days she had performed as organist with a measure of credit. She was to discharge this function again on the great day.

No thought whatever had been given to how I would fit into the proceedings and, I calculate that, to this very day, the Prout family is oblivious of my painful participation.

Trouble began when my romp in the barn with the two dogs was abruptly interrupted.

"You'm to pump the organ," I was told by Aunt Annie.

It was as though I had been singled out for some mysterious

commission which might have dreadful consequences like preaching a sermon or even shearing a sheep.

"I 'ent no good at that," I said, "Can't yer get some won else?"

But it was all to no avail. The committee had decided I was to pump the organ. And what was more, I was to start right away with a practice run!

In no time at all, I was being led firmly by the hand out of the back door and into the garden. As we followed the path I was told in a very firm voice what I had to do. I do not know whether Aunt Annie thought I might bolt at any minute but she continued to grip my hand as in a vice. Even when we reached the Gothic door which led us into the churchyard she contrived to keep me a prisoner, spilling sheets of music on the ground in the process.

In picking up the music, Aunt Annie caught her toe in the front of her long lace dress and almost pitched to the ground. Accordingly, she was in no happy mood as we passed the Prout family graves and proceeded into the church.

In the dimly lit building, the pace did not slacken until we reached the organ stationed in the chancel. A chequered pattern of coloured mosaic illuminated the altar cloth as the sunlight strained through the leaded East window.

As the ringing of my boots on the tiled floor died away, my hand was released. It would prove useless to run away now, so I stood nervously waiting.

The organ was rather like a double-yolked piano. It seemed to have two of everything. Besides this, there were pedals underneath and a host of round and square pipes coming out of the top. I would need at least two pairs of hands to cope with this fearsome instrument.

But my part did not involve anything technical, just a measure of continuous hard graft as I was soon to learn.

On the secluded side of the organ extended a long wooden handle which, when moved up and down, inflated the bellows. I was committed to become the motive power and Aunt Annie gave me clear instruction to this effect.

I grasped the handle with both hands and was immediately alarmed to find how difficult it was to move. It needed every ounce of my meagre strength to push it upwards and all my swinging body weight to pull it down. Even so, I could not operate the full extent of the upwards movement. I just was not tall enough, so I was provided with a prayer stool to stand on. By stepping on and off the stool I managed, with considerable effort, to produce the wind pressure.

Then I was shown a pressure gauge on the wall above my head. It was a very simple contraption. A needle which moved, up and down, a scale which had two fixed indicating points. At the top a line which showed that there was sufficient wind and at the bottom a line which indicated that there was not enough. I must keep the needle safely between the two to avoid trouble.

My aunt started to play the organ and the needle began to fall, so frantically I began pumping and the needle moved upwards. Then she pulled out some stops and the organ started to roar and the needle fell rapidly. Only a superhuman effort on my part kept the needle hovering above the bottom line. When I thought that all was lost, the stops were pushed back in and the needle moved upwards again.

I began to realise that I was involved in a life and death struggle. A contest against the diapason. If I failed in my purpose, then all music must cease and shame would fall on me.

For upwards of an hour my aunt continued to play the organ and for upwards of an hour I provided the wind. Then, finally, my aunt decided the practice was over and, in an almost collapsed state, I returned the prayer-stool to its pew.

We walked less briskly back through the churchyard. Perhaps it would not be quite so bad to be dead, I thought, as we filtered through the graves. But once back in the large Court kitchen an ample helping of rice pudding at least partially revived me.

"How did you get on then?" enquired Aunt Emily.

"Bit strange at first after so long," said Aunt Annie.

"And how about young Ken?" continued Aunt Emily.

"Oh, he did quite well," replied Aunt Annie. "But time enough for compliments after tomorrow."

If it were possible for my heart to sink further it must have fallen from my boots. Surely my task was over. They would never trust me to perform on the great day.

I knew it would be useless to argue so I must go sick or something in the morning.

Maybe Aunt Emily anticipated this reaction on my part, because when she came to call me next morning she had a large bar of chocolate which she dangled in front of my nose. Temporarily, my painful thoughts left me and when the chocolate was eaten, I found myself fully clothed with little hope that subtlety would be successful. I was beaten.

A lifetime passed before the Standish bells began to ring and even then it would be a good half hour until I was again in purgatory.

Grandmother and cousins, aunts and uncles milled all around me in their Sunday-best attire. And then, with prayer-books in hand, a procession wound its way through the garden and churchyard into the holy building now bedecked with all manner of fruit and vegetables.

Again, I was led by the arm up the nave and into the chancel. This was my final scaffold, I must try to be brave unto the very end.

My aunt gave me a gentle push around the corner as she slid onto the organ bench. And then suddenly there was salvation.

For it was Sam Harris. Grinning down on me as a golden sun following a black storm and I collapsed in the warmth of delirious reinforcement.

"Yer Aunt Emily asked I ter giv' 'e an' 'and," he whispered hoarsely, "an' I 'new it were 'ard goin' fer a nipper loike thee!"

"So you wants t'ze 'em then," said Sam Harris, as he replaced the single egg which the nest contained and the unhooked himself from a fierce bramble growing beneath a pear tree in the orchard. "Well I 'ent got all that menie, but thick 'un is just av'ridge an' won't be no good in my collectshun. If we de go 'ome right away ye kin 'av a look afore tea.''

I did not need a second bidding because the beautiful egg I had just seen filled me with wonderment. It was about the size of a small walnut, as blue as the brightest sky in summer and peppered with fine black spots.

It was put back into a nest which was beautifully woven from the stems of dead plants and grass and had a paste lining of wood pith which simulated delicate cardboard.

To see more of such prize objects was an experience which had great appeal, so I trotted briskly away with my rustic friend whose legs were twice the length of mine.

It was but three hundred yards to Sam's snug cottage home where dwelt the large family of Ephraim and Clara Harris. How so many souls found hostel in this little stone dwelling place was a secret retained by the family alone. Maybe the outside world chose to be oblivious. Who should care how upwards of a dozen bodies lay each night, if there was no complaint when two bedrooms alone were available.

Sam ducked under a festooning branch of a pear tree whose trunk paralleled the cottage wall and we gained access inside through the stable-type door which was ever open at the top. The dim interior was paved with uneven stone slabbing which sloped and buckled. The walls and ceiling were uniform yellow ochre produced by years of cooking and tobacco smoke. Several faded pictures completed the scene but these were so covered with a misty grey film that the subjects they framed could scarcely be seen. Wooden table and chairs were there in plenty, polished smooth in exposed places by the clothes of the family which used them. A baby's railed cot stood in a corner and a fire flickered in a black iron range.

Clara Harris was laying the table with plates of many shapes and patterns and her left hand grasped a bundle of steel knives whose handles bore scars of the frying pan.

''Well, well!'' she said as we entered, ''And for whot am I 'onoured by this visit?''

''EE's cum ter zee my yegs,'' replied Sam.

"If that's wot you'm up to then you best take 'um outside. Yer cun zee I be busy gettin' tea. Mind an' be careful 'ow yer get's 'um down. They'm on top of cuppered upstairs wer yer put 'em."

Sam opened a door in the corner of the room and disappeared up a steep wooden staircase having first shed his boots. Nobody was allowed on the floor above except when footwear had been removed. I heard noises above which indicated that a chair was being placed in front of the cupboard and then Sam re-appeared carrying a wooden box.

He went straight through the room and out into the garden without stopping to put on his boots. I was immediately behind Sam when he placed the box on an old wooden bench under one of the cottage windows.

I stood transfixed. Never before in my young life had I seen an egg collection. My wildest dreams of Sam's had not accommodated anything so splendid.

The box was about two feet square with sides six inches deep. It had a hinged lid of framed glass, the whole stained and varnished. A layer of fine sawdust covered the bottom and in this were embedded rows of eggs of many colours, shapes and sizes. The large eggs were at the top and the small eggs at the bottom. There were blue eggs and brown eggs, green eggs and white eggs. Some with spots and some with blotches. Some were matt and some were glossy. Right in the middle was a round egg as red as blood. Near it was a brown mottled egg which had its small end sharply pointed.

Sam painstakingly named the eggs for me, row by row, and when all was done I was a little wiser. Three things emerged from that first contact with Sam's eggs. Firstly, that the blood red egg had been laid by a kestrel; secondly, that the mottled brown egg had been laid by a peewit; and thirdly, I resolved that I must start to collect a box full of these treasures for myself.

Having now put on his boots, Sam saw me safely back to the Court and handed me over to Aunt Emily who listened attentively to my exaggerated description of what I had just seen. She smiled whimsically as my emotions carried me further and further from the truth but she did not deny my excited prattle. What did it really matter that I had not been to the British Museum? Best let young Ken get the excitement out of his system. If she could help, of course she would, and indeed she did by providing a suitable cardboard box, complete with a layer of bran in the bottom.

Then came my bedtime.

I carried my oological receptacle upstairs and placed it with great care on the dressing-table. In my mind it already contained such priceless articles that made careless handling quite out of the question.

I lay awake long after the candle had disappeared from my bedroom, the deadly silence broken only by a rat gnawing at the wooden joists below the floor. I had long since learnt to accept such noises as normal and it would have taken something of far greater consequence to interrupt my excited cogitation.

I found myself trying to account for all the kinds of birds I knew and I soon became confused with the big black ones. The little brown ones presented an even greater problem and it soon became very obvious to me that without Sam to help I would make little progress. Sam then must be my tutor, at least for the time being, and with this very satisfactory thought, I fell asleep.

All young boys dream, possibly because they persist in eating the wrong things before they go to bed.

My subconscious mind did not fail to react to the piece of cheese I had consumed with my supper, with rewarding result.

I climbed tall trees for eggs; I swam in big ponds for eggs; and I searched in thick tangles for eggs. I found rare eggs and common eggs, big eggs and little eggs.

Then I awoke in a cold sweat before my appointed hour because, as is so typical of all my pleasant dreams, they have a habit of turning sour. I had suddenly discovered that my entire night's collection had been eaten by the rats.

In the half-light, I sat bolt upright in bed and as I did so, one of these rodents jumped to the floor from the dressing table. The bran was too great a temptation and there was a hole in the side of Aunt Emily's cardboard box!

This happening was perhaps a blessing in disguise. It taught me to exercise the greatest possible care in protecting the things which I cherished.

But, at the time, animosity swelled within me against the creatures which had destroyed the very beginnings of my egg collection.

Torn between anger and despair, I was very miserable when Aunt Emily came into my room to bid me get up. She had every sympathy when she saw what had happened and she lost no time in supplying a further box complete with bran.

My enthusiasm had returned by the time Sam arrived at the kitchen door.

"I'de think I can get yer a magpie te' staart yer collectshun," he said with some excitement. "Not very 'igh in a thorn 'edge by the Mill. Miller White shaud 'un to I an' sed I best smash th' eggs afore 'um 'atches."

Smash eggs! This was unthinkable. How could anyone do such a thing when they were so priceless? Sam must rescue these eggs just as quickly as possible! I was certain the magpie would approve.

I ran beside Sam who walked faster than usual in the direction of the old Mill.

Miller White poked his head around the door as we drew near.

"I thought twer a pony a trottin' wen I 'urd yer," he smiled. "Was expectin' a mon fram Stonehouse just."

The miller stepped out onto the massive stone slab, four feet above the ground and at the top of a flight of well-worn steps which formed a platform for the wagons of grain. Then he patiently filled a stumpy clay pipe with tobacco from a highly polished tin on which little of the original advertisement remained. His gnarled finger and thumb extracted a box of matches from a waistcoat pocket and a cloud of smoke engulfed his white powdered head before he spoke again.

"Ye'll be ader thick magpie, I'll be bound. Mind 'e done rip yer trousers.''

And he chuckled heartily as he removed the pipe from his mouth to spit into a bunch of stinging nettles.

Sam and I paused only long enough to avoid a breach of protocol and then hurried down the lane.

We clambered over a five-barred gate into a field and then climbed a grassy bank along a very thick blackthorn hedge. Sam stopped suddenly and peered up into the top of the hedge where I saw a mass of sticks, round like a football.

"I wunder if 'urs on,'' he said, picking up a loose sod of earth which he proceeded to hurl at the nest. His aim was accurate and the missile disintegrated with quite a splatter as it collided with the sticks. Immediately, a magpie departed from a hole in the side of the nest, dropping like a stone and then veering away in a piebald flutter.

Sam lost no time in clambering up the ten feet necessary, accompanied by a measure of grunting and a few choice swear words as the thorn spikes scratched his hands and prodded his buttocks. It took the full length of his arm to probe the innermost secret. With his head twisted sideways in an abortive attempt to avoid a sharp thorn which succeeded in impaling his ear, Sam announced, "Urs got zix!''

Excitedly, I watched Sam transfer each egg in turn to the comparative safety of his jacket pocket, then he very carefully climbed back down. He extracted himself from the middle of the hedge with parts of it adorning his tattered clothing and then he knelt gingerly down, spreading his handkerchief on the grass as he did so.

One by one, the magpie eggs were laid down on the handkerchief. I stood transfixed as I watched.

"Them's good 'uns,'' said Sam as he examined each in some detail. "We'll 'ave dree each.'' "But I best blow you'rn fer thee.''

He stood up and then carefully selected a sharp spike from a blackthorn branch with which he made a hole in each end of an egg. Holding it to his mouth with thumb and forefinger, he blew out the contents onto the ground.

I was now completely lost in admiration and obediently held out my hands to receive my share of the spoil. Once before in my young life and had I been given a bird's egg by Sam; now I had three which were far more valuable.

Before I went to bed that night, I watched Aunt Emily secure these treasures in their cardboard box which she placed in the mahogany sideboard in the dining room.

"No rat will get in there," she said.

And so my bad dream did not return!

Chapter six
Parkend Lodge Farm

I somehow felt, as I got out of bed, that it was going to be a thoroughly satisfactory day. A little bee had caught itself behind the glass of my open bedroom window and this I guided out into the sunshine with the aid of a comb picked up from the dressing table. In the cow-yard below two newly-born calves frolicked over the heaps of manure not yet carried to the fields while their mothers yielded to the brown hands of Ephraim and Tom in the adjoining cow stalls.

On a nearby roof two pigeons wrenched their necks up and down with their bills locked together and the swifts screeched as they flashed wildly in excited arcs around the stables.

There was so much going on outside that I must hasten to become involved.

It took me little time to dress and less to wash. Breakfast was but a fast gulping formality and I was out in the sun.

"You'm just in time for a ride," said Uncle Robert as though he was well aware of the speed with which my bed and I had separated. "We'm off to Parkend to see yer Uncle Oswald so jump in quick."

I needed no second bidding and was hoisted by the arm up into the 'buggy'.

George Hughes had been holding the reins close to the bit in the pony's mouth and when he saw me safely settled on the canvas seat he too leapt on board. Now it was Diamond's turn and he also reacted to the splendid morning. A fast trot alternated with a jerking canter which made it necessary for George Hughes to tighten the reins and jump to his feet several times.

"Steady now!" he shouted at the pony as he jerked the

leathers. "What's got in yer?" Then he glanced at Uncle Robert and said, "He 'ant 'ad no oats this mornin'. Can't unnerstannd wot's cum over 'im."

But the excitement was short-lived and soon we were trotting briskly down the lane to the Bristol road. We passed several farms and a number of cottages on our way and at most of these we were either waved to or shouted at. Katie and Mary Jenner came running round from the back of the house, in pale blue dresses and straw pudding-basin hats. I blushed purple when Uncle Robert said, "Which ov they pretty twins be'ye goin' to marry, Ken?"

To add to my complete discomfort George Hughes, with a twinkle in his eye, put a tight rein on the pony and we came to a standstill. The Jenner twins came running out into the lane and without invitation were soon scrambling into the 'buggy'.

"Now ye can taake yer pick," chided Uncle Robert, scarcely able to conceal his mirth. "They'm real pretty, ain't they?"

While perhaps I was inclined to agree, at that very moment my only desire was to get as far away as possible. But there was no escape, so I buried my face in the padded cushion, exposing the soles of my boots and the rounded part of my pants to the young ladies.

The two men now roared with laughter when one of the twins said, "Ain't ee silly!" and the other added, "Most boys are, but I likes 'em best with blue eyes!"

Few Prouts had eyes of any other colour but mine remained concealed until Uncle Robert changed my position with a deft pinch with his thumb and finger in a place where it hurt me most.

When my ostrich head was again able to take stock of the situation, I was relieved to find that the girls' mother was walking down the garden path towards us. She laughed heartily as she grabbed a daughter in either hand and then, when each was held against her shapely figure she chided, "Two at a time's a bit much fer young Ken it seems!"

It was Diamond who shortened my embarrassment by suddenly jerking forward, catching us all off balance. George

Hughes rather than admit that he was not in control, made a 'chucking' noise, jerked the reins, and we were away down the lane once more.

And then it all happened. We were not twenty yards away from the Bristol road, when Uncle Robert shouted, ''Just look at that!''

As George Hughes once again reined Diamond to a standstill, there came trundling along the main road a vehicle which had no horses. It was a big navy-blue thing which towered above us. It had doors all along its side and people sat in rows waving at us. Some even stood up and shouted above the noise of the engine which roared at the front. Massive cast iron wheels, clad with solid rubber two inches thick, scraunched the gritty road. The pilot in front was a man in a smart peaked cap adorned with a white linen covering and goggles.

We sat transfixed for some minutes as the monster disappeared towards Whitminster in a cloud of dust and smoke. When only a feint rumbling remained, Uncle Robert turned to me, his face alight, and said ''Well young Ken, you've seen yer furst!''

And indeed I had. Many a time since I have wondered whether it was a good thing or not!

A charabanc outing of the period.
[Leyland Bus courtesy Transport Publishing Company]

I am sure that Diamond also had difficulty in deciding what manner of creature he had just encountered for he too watched the whole proceeding with his ears cocked well to the front. Had not George Hughes reined Diamond to the right his enquiring mind would have directed a left turn. And even when we trotted away in a Gloucester direction, Diamond's ears swivelled first to the front and then to the rear. However, once in Parkend Lane and off the Bristol road, all was forgotten.

The lane was but wide enough for the 'buggy' but occasionally there was a passing place. The hedges were dense and lush on either side and a clear water ditch hugged a shallow grass verge. A metallic dragonfly hovered above the water and then darted, fast as light, to a pendent station near a clump of rush.

On a spiky blackthorn, a yellow hammer jangled his monotonous song — "a little bit of bread and no cheeze."

Away down the lane we espied the 'carrier' from Saul. He was waiting for us in a passing place near a field gateway and, as we drew nearer, Uncle Robert slipped from the 'buggy' to lead Diamond, whose ears again twitched nervously. Once broadside we stopped.

The driver, a thick-set, ruddy-faced man with curly grey mutton-chop whiskers, raised a bowler hat, green with age and said, "Mornin' Mister Robert, Jarge and yung bhoy. Vine dey ent it." Both my companions agreed and then Uncle Robert said, "Got room fer a sack of seed spuds to Glo'ster on Saaterday, Mister Dangerfield?"

"Aah I de think zo," said the driver and then the two men set about arranging the details.

I was far more interested in the box van which I could almost touch if I reached out my hand. It was shabby black with a convex roof which was stacked with odd bags and boxes, each well tied to a surrounding guardrail.

A square window on either side illuminated an interior which had two long seats served by a central gangway. Two steps, securely bracketed at the rear, assisted a passenger to enter, but only half a door could be closed behind and this had a large brass handle. Most of the weight was carried on a pair of tall but slender wheels and a smaller pair supported the driver's seat up front. Every available inch of the bodywork was used for advertisement, much hand-painted and bleached by the summer sun. But some areas were reserved for stick-on bills which told of fat-stock sales, bell-ringing contests and a new brand of embrocation for rheumatic pain.

Diamond looked puny beside the beautiful chestnut animal, deserving a more stately employment, but what Stallard lacked in dignity did not detract from his muscular opulence. He scarcely acknowledged the smaller pony but Diamond persisted in trying to bite the larger animal. I think he must have succeeded had not Uncle Robert maintained a tight rein.

The arrangements for the delivery of 'the seed spuds' were made and we were on our way once again. Dangerfield and his 'carrier' would be involved in many such deals before Gloucester was reached, much later in the day.

Our journey was now completed. Hardly was the 'carrier' out of sight when we reached a large hay-barn. This was the beginning of Parkend Lodge Farm and, at the bottom of the drive, the gate was open. Diamond took his time walking up the slope to the farmhouse where Uncle Oswald, and cousins Ronnie and Basil, were waiting for us.

We were greeted in our arrival by a continuous chorus of baas, set in every imaginable pitch and produced by a flock of sheep, close penned in an adjoining yard. Upwards of a hundred larynxes performed this discordant symphony which all but drowned the greetings of our relatives.

The woolly animals standing closest to the gate gazed at us through cynical, pale yellow eyes, offering no compromise. We humans just were not trusted and their nervous bodies panted in the torment of the hot summer sun.

Some of their number were already wandering disconsolately in a much larger compound where they had been released after treatment, but still making spontaneous contribution to the unconducted orchestra.

Tom Davis and Charlie Markie were the maggot hunters. Each sheep in turn was grabbed by a pair of swarthy hands whose curving fingers probed deep into the greasy fleece. Keen eyes searched wool along the back, above the tail and throughout the manure matted hind-quarters. If maggots were found, then liquid from a bottle that looked like cold tea, was applied and rubbed in until it frothed. Soon the helpless maggots, like rice from a pudding, were falling to the ground and the raw flesh of the unfortunate sheep was relieved of its chewing torment.

One by one the animals were examined and one by one they were lifted bodily and swung over a low rail to be released into the larger compound. Each, as it found its feet, seemed surprised to be free and, whether through temerity or exultation it commenced to baa.

For a while we sat watching in the 'buggy', thoroughly intrigued by the nonchalant skill with which the sheep were handled.

Then Uncle Oswald said, ''An' whot about a drop of zider!'' So we all trooped to the cool of the cellar.

For the very young, the cider-cellar had no great attraction. It was only the older folk who, once in, found it difficult to come out.

Ronnie, Basil and I had not reached an age of compulsion, so we were able, after each had taken a healthy draught, to emerge in good condition for other things.

Birds' nesting!

My cousins knew where there was a starling's nest. Their own collection was already supplied with the eggs of most birds which nested around the farm and so a starling's egg could be mine for the taking. It would not be difficult to get and certainly, no grown-up need be involved.

The route was simple. Ronnie led the way, Basil followed and I took my place at the rear. First we entered the stable and crossed the cobbled floor past the rear end of a tethered cart horse. Then along the stone wall at his side with barely sufficient room to reach the manger. The right toe into a hole vacated conveniently by a stone and up among the hay and the snorting nostrils of the horse. Next we hoisted ourselves through a gap left by a missing wooden spar in the crib above and finally, to the upper floor via the provender slot in the boarding.

Now there was little light to guide us save that piercing the gaps in the random stone tiling. We must be careful to pick our steps as the partly rotten floor is well sprinkled with hay. Step where there was a beam underneath and all would be well. It was the half-way position where danger lay as could be seen by a number of jagged holes made by previous erring boots. But navigation was good and we crossed safely to the far gable-end, avoiding two sets of oak braces and king-posts in the process. Just within reach, and where a purlin entered the stonework, was a narrow gap under the tiles.

In a cavity beyond this, with a further hole to the outside air, the starling had her nest.

Standing on tiptoe, Ronnie inserted his hand and an external fluttering indicated that the brooding bird was making a hasty get-away.

"She's got a nest-full," said Ronnie, withdrawing his hand. "You feel," he continued, turning to me.

I pushed my hand through the gap under the tiles and, as I did so, I experienced a measure of timidity lest the ends of my fingers should be bitten by a rat or some other wild creature. But the warmth of the nest reassured me and my excitement rose as the tips of my fingers touched the eggs.

"How many 'as 'er got then?" enquired one of my cousins.

"I'll try an' count," I said.

But this was not easy as the nest was a mass of feathers and straw and I was none too good at arithmetic anyway.

"I'll get one out," I said.

As space did not permit me to close my hand, I manipulated an egg between the ends of my two longest fingers and pre-cariously eased it towards me. After a few inches, I was able to obtain a more positive hold and with a little careful juggling my prize was safely extracted.

Even though the light was dim, the delicate pale blue egg filled me with wonderment. The colour of the sky on a sunny summer day and yet, with a slight translucence, tinted by the bright orange yolk within. A beauty short-lived, to be lost under the breast of the starling or, maybe, as a drying shell in my collection box. Only successful blowing would determine the latter.

But now Ronnie must try to count the eggs we left for the bird. Basil and I watched him as again on tiptoe he felt into the nest.

"There be at least vore," he pronounced, and in that statement he was probably correct.

So we retraced our steps to the open air, the starling egg in my hand undamaged by the clambering journey.

Having proudly exhibited the priceless gem to the cider-drinkers in the cellar, it was found temporary storage on an old saucer in the kitchen window.

Upon our return it soon became apparent that my two uncles had discussed the immediate future.

"Yer de seem to be enjoyin' yerself, young Ken," said Uncle Robert. "Ow would yer loike ter staay with yer cousins fer a daay er two? Uncle Oswald says 'twill be alright."

And the two uncles nodded to each other approvingly.

"Yer Aunt Emily will be glad to see the back of yer fer a bit," grinned Uncle Oswald.

Both uncles watched for my reaction and I am sure they would have been surprised had it been anything other than immediate elation. To remain with Ronnie and Basil would certainly be too wonderful for words and besides they were awful good at birds' nesting.

I lost no time in signifying my complete acceptance and the three of us ran shouting into the farmhouse to tell Aunt Edith that her family had increased.

Not that Aunt Edith would consider the matter of any consequence for she was accustomed to entertain at short notice swarms of hay-makers, cider-drinkers and shooting-parties who had a habit of requiring food and lodging at all sorts of odd times.

80

Aunt Edith rubbed her hard-worked fingers through my untidy hair and then playfully smacked me on the bottom.

"'Twill be quite alright so long as you don't want more'n four eggs and a pound ov bacon fer yer breakfast," she chuckled. "Now run along, all of you, and don't get into mischief!"

I suppose, for the very first time in my life, I experienced a new freedom. Usually, there was someone older than myself keeping a watchful eye. Ronnie and Basil, though younger in age, were mature and I had much to learn from them.

We pushed open a creaking white paled gate which admitted us to a well-kept garden. Row upon row of onion, potato and cabbage stretched away from the well-trodden earth path. Here and there a damson tree and against a wall an elderly William pear, its branches following the powdered joints in the mellow brickwork. A small forest of blackcurrant bushes was separated from a thicket of hazel by an orderly patch of strawberry plants. This half-acre providing the luxury of country life, by no means always available elsewhere.

It was not a question of stolen fruit today, however, because, apart from the odd strawberry which disappeared when we were certain that nobody was watching, we had other far more important things to do.

Firstly, we must inspect the tame rabbits.

Against a sheltered but sunny wall stood a row of boxes with mesh wire fronts, their floors well covered with hay. A long narrow shelf supported with legs, held all at a convenient height.

One by one, each rabbit was lifted gingerly by its ears through a small door secured with hinges of rough leather strapping. It was then placed for examination on the top of its box.

My cousins proudly provided a complete case-history of each rabbit. Its name, its sex, its age and its origin. Some were home-bred and some had been bought, two were gifts and an old buck had been exchanged.

A rough valuation was produced in typical farming fashion

and the fingers of both hands were used for the purpose. When all was done, and there were no fingers left, it was decided that the stock-value was in excess of ten shillings.

At this point, Aunt Edith came hurrying out to us, she always did everything half as fast again as most people and, placing an old bucket on the ground, she said "What about the stray hens' nest then?"

Although I had yet to learn, my cousins knew immediately what was required of us. We were to go birds' nesting — officially!

Aunt Edith said she had concrete evidence that two Rhode Island Reds had stolen nests in the 'wood-pile' and she was also certain that a White Leghorn had a nest in a hole in a large straw rick — "Between the boultins."

Our simple commission was a bucket full of hens eggs. Ronnie picked up the bucket and Basil and I followed him through the small gate at the bottom of the garden into the orchard. Thirty yards further on and we came to the 'wood-pile'.

Maybe the name is adeqaute to describe the accumulation of forty tons of firewood, but perhaps it is as well to explain that the fire-wood covered a considerable area and was no-where higher than three feet. Some of this timber nearest the hedge was in a well rotted condition because it had not been reached before the winter was at an end. A fresh supply had then been added in front with the advent of warmer weather.

All manner of weeds and a limited amount of bramble were growing up through the fire-wood and, of course, there were nettles, nettles and more nettles.

In the centre of a bare patch covered with sawdust and chippings, stood a solid wooden saw-bench grey-grained and with lichen legs. Several young rabbits retreated into the jungle of gnarled branches and rank vegetation as we reached the perimeter.

As though well accustomed to the required procedure, Ronnie and Basil pulled the sleeves of their grey woollen jerseys down over their hands and commenced to clamber over the fire-wood like a pair of young apes. Thumbs and fore-fingers gripped the sleeve at its edge and the encased knuckles, while protected from the stinging nettles, were used to assist in balance.

It was note long before a hen's nest was found. It was less than a yard inside the wood-pile and it held two layers of brown eggs. I participated with great excitement in the human chain which passed the eggs by hand the short distance to the waiting bucket.

Once again, my cousins' greater knowledge was brought to bear. An egg was broken and its contents examined.

"Fresh as paint," was the verdict.

Now stimulated by success, my early reluctance to clamber left me and I found myself, rather nervously, penetrating the wood-pile.

It was 'beginner's luck' when I looked down into the nettles and saw a nest which held far more eggs than I could count. I shouted to my cousins who, once again, joined in the extracting procedure. However, this time the eggs were not placed in the bucket immediately, but laid in the grass at the edge of the wood-pile.

"Must test won fust," said Ronnie.

Then he glanced mischievously at his younger brother and challenged, "Bet yer can't swaller won 'ole!"

Basil, as I was to learn later in life, never accepted second place to Ronnie, and immediately retorted, "I'll bet won ov my white does fer yer black buck!"

"Go on, let's see yer then," chided his older brother.

With an air of calculated determination, Basil took out his pocket knife and made a deft slash in the blunt end of an egg. Then, bending his neck until he almost fell over backwards, he tipped the contents of an egg into his mouth. His cheeks bulged as his lips came together and he stood motionless for a few moments with his eyes staring. It was obvious that the egg filled Basil's mouth to overflowing and when he attempted to gulp it down his throat, it just would not go. The yolk was still intact in its sac and was far too large to slide down my small cousin's gullet. Basil's face lost its pinkish flush and turned a pale grey-green which darkened with each abortive attempt to swallow.

Ronnie did not alleviate his brother's predicament when he suggested, "I'll bet 'uns addled!"

But Basil, in spite of his obvious discomfort, was determined that the egg should go down the way he intended and continued to gulp like an old hen with the croup. His arms, well bent at the elbows, simulated a pair of wings as they pumped up and down, in unison with his attempts to swallow. He became even more grey-green, his eyes stood out on his cheeks and we thought that at any second he must expire.

Then, just when all appeared to be lost, there was a minor explosion, the yolk broke and the orange-yellow fluid oozed from the from the sides of Basil's mouth and dripped down onto his jersey.

It goes without saying that the rabbits remained in their original ownership. Basil contended that he had swallowed most of the egg, while Ronnie was equally certain that by far the greater portion had dripped off Basil's chin.

The nest of the Leghorn presented no serious problem. My cousins soon clambered up onto the straw-rick and discovered a nest full of large white eggs tucked away down between two 'boultins'. In turn, after test, were these eggs added to those already in the bucket and, with a sense of accomplishment, I went with my two cousins back to the farm kitchen. Here, Aunt Edith paid compliment for our success before informing us that "Dinner is ready!"

News of this welcome event had obviously reached the maggoters as the scraunch of hobnails on the paving-flags outside gave notice that the morning's work was done.

The pump under the lean-to roof was brought into action. Ample pulsations of water discharged into the hewn-stone trough, a large red tablet of 'Lifebuoy' soap slopped in and out of an open wooden box nailed to the wall and the roller towel rattled on the back door.

George Hughes, Uncle Robert, Charlie Markie, Tom

Davis and finally Uncle Oswald with two newcomers trooped into the room.

There followed a short period when chairs rattled and scraped over the stone floor as the hungry multitude ranged itself around the massive linen-covered table. From the dark interior of an ample kitchen range, whose hinges, top and fastenings shone with polished steel, was drawn a brown sizzling baron of beef. The large oval serving dish which supported this great piece of meat ruckled the tablecloth as it slid into position in front of Uncle Oswald.

"Rost bif an' Yarkzire pud," confirmed George Hughes, half-dribbling, his eyes alight, as a large metal tray of Yorkshire pudding was ranged close at hand.

Soon the centre of the table was weighted down with dishes of potatoes and 'greens' and tureens of gravy and ''oss radish sawse'.

A stack of a dozen dinner-plates reduced, one by one, until there was none and concurrently, piles of food appeared in the empty spaces in front of each person. When all had been served, Uncle Oswald laid the carving knife and fork on the dish and said happily, "Done wait, get stuck in."

Conversation stopped and the noise of serious mastication took its place.

Such was a countryman's Sunday Dinner. Little or nothing remained in any dish and the washing-up process was thereby facilitated. In any case this undertaking was the province of the womenfolk. As far as Parkend Lodge Farm was concerned it would be Aunt Edith and Daisy Brooks who would bear the drudgery. Cousin Eileen was not yet old enough to take her part but her time would soon come.

The repast finished, the Standish 'buggy' homeward bound, the pots and pans cleared away and then began the only part of the week when rest was permitted in daylight hours.

An old rug was spread on the lawn beneath the red May tree, a pipe 'ov' baccy' and then 'a couple ov' 'ours ov' kip'. Only the bright green caterpillar dangling on a gossamer of silk and the buzzing yellow wasp to cause distraction.

If one indulged then stillness was the order. For my cousins and I, escape to further adventure just as soon as snores gave permission.

Maybe the grown-ups were little concerned at our departure. Perhaps they were glad to be rid of the risk of disturbance and the necessity to administer reprimand. So we clambered un-molested over the railings which separated the garden from the 'front-ground' and made our way across the cow-rutted turf to the 'moat'. If a castle was associated with this sheet of water then no stonework remained to tell the tale. I strongly suspect that some romantic swain of yester-year had decided he pre-ferred the name to pond. But water of any sort is romantic to small boys and my cousins and I were no exception.

Generally during daytime the 'moat' was the headquarters of the farmhouse grey geese and 'rudder' ducks. They swam over its extensive surface chattering to each other all the while and occasionally they broke forth in exultation with much more noisy babbling. Patches of green pond-weed like neat billiard-tables covered much of the 'dead' water while pollarded wil-lows dangled their lower fronds in the shaded corners. In several places the banks and water-edges were obliterated by large bramble bushes and there were sloppy, muddy places where the cows went down to drink. A cluster of mature and stately elms filtered the sunlight onto the sparkling water.

Here was fascination for the adult and adventure for the young.

As we reached the water's edge a moorhen slipped from her nest and, with jerking neck, hurried her way to the shelter of an overhanging bramble, leaving behind her a vee of ripple on the otherwise mirror surface. The neat dishing of flotsam and dead reed which held her oatmeal eggs was supported on a partly submerged branch of willow which stretched over deep water.

My cousins and I stood on the bank looking enviously at a prize which appeared far beyond our reach.

Then Ronnie had a brilliant idea.

He would go back to the garden and get a kidney bean stick and tie a table spoon to the end. If he took off his boots and stockings and waded out as far as he could, he was confident that the eggs could be reached. The water was quite shallow near the bank and the rest would be easy.

In no time at all he had returned to the moat with a stick to which part of the kidney bean was still entwined. He had 'borrowed' a large silver spoon from the dining room.

Ronnie took off his boots and with one of the laces he tied the spoon to the thin end of the bean-stick and then he removed his stockings and rolled up his short trousers tightly onto his thighs.

Fascinated, Basil and I watched as Ronnie, the stick held firmly in both hands, moved gingerly to the edge of the pond. Determination written all over his face. He sat down on the bank and dangled his white feet in the water. The sudden chill sapped his courage a little because, kicking his legs up and down, he said, "I best cool 'em down a bit or I might get th' cramp."

It seemed quite a time before Ronnie moved again and just when we thought the attempt was on the point of failure Ronnie suddenly slipped off the edge of the bank into the water and mud up to his waist. He made a gasping vocal sound as he threw his arms into the air, dropping the bean-stick in the process. Then he floundered about like a drunken man as his feet became engulfed in the mud. For several seconds he struggled to regain his balance and even when the risk of total collapse had disappeared, Ronnie found difficulty in preventing his legs from sliding under him.

Now thoroughly splashed and splattered with mud on the half of his body which remained above water, he moved gingerly sideways to regain possession of the bean-stick which was floating steadily away from him. Even the act of reaching for this almost brought calamity but, once again, danger passed and Ronnie prepared himself for the final onslaught.

With bean-stick floating in the water and pointing towards the nest, now some ten feet away, he inched his way forward.

The rather insecure 'handrail' still adorned with the red flowers of a kidney bean.

Steadily the distance between Ronnie and his objective shortened until the end of the bean-stick was within two feet of the nest. By this time the water had risen to my cousin's arm-pits.

And then, just when success appeared within Ronnie's grasp, the horrible truth was exposed.

As the end of the bean-stick touched the moorhen's nest, it was discovered that the silver spoon was no longer attached!

Later in the day, the moorhen returned to continue incubating her eggs, no doubt unaware that somewhere in the mud below her was a large silver spoon etched with the letter 'P' for Prout.

Long before the adults had terminated their period of relaxation to commence the afternoon milking, Ronnie had paid a secret visit to the pump. Here the mud was removed as far as possible and then we walked out into the sunshine to allow his shirt and trousers to dry.

I suspect that a time arrived when Aunt Edith found herself short of a silver spoon but whether she had any idea of the circumstance surrounding its loss I shall now never know.

Parkend Lodge Farm   **[Courtesy Mrs E. Tranter]**

Chapter seven
Castle Bridge

Our return to the farm buildings found the evening milking well in hand and scant attention was paid to us, which was all to the good. The brief break from farm work was ended for another week. While it lasted, the rest was most acceptable, but now the cows needed attention and they must not wait.

Cecil Hewer grinned at us as we entered the cow-stalls, his head adorned with an old trilby hat, flattened over his forehead and well polished with hair and animal grease. He carried a large galvanised bucket filled with warm froth, a trouser-polished three-legged stool which had a spall missing from the seat and he wore a long apron which was damp at the bottom.

"Only 'leven more then 'ome," he told us. "Yer aunt was askin' wer yer was."

We watched a while as Daisy yielded her milk to the square brown hands of Tom Davis. She appeared quite happy to be relieved of her heavy burden. Her contented eyes shaded with long lashes, watched us in unconcerned satisfaction. Every now and then a round ball belched up her throat which she patiently chewed until the procedure was repeated. Occasionally she flicked her tail across Tom's back and intermittently raised a hind leg which Tom wristed away from the bucket.

In the well-partitioned end stall we found Bill. His broad expanse of coarse hair and tapering horns thumped the timber beams which secured him. The polished metal chain around his neck rattled through a stout steel ring as he tossed his head in challenge. This first excitement gone, he sniffed and snozzled at us until the copper ring through his nose rose into a vertical position. Then, the bovine inquisition exhausted, he stood quite still as we made our way out into the yard.

Nancy, 'the moke', was here to meet us. She spent her life with the cows because it was said that a female donkey running with them prevented the 'wharp'. The eating of a certain weed caused the early loss of embryo. Nancy prevented this by eating all the obnoxious growth and the cows held their calves until the appointed time — or so the countryfolk claimed!

In any event, the theory provided my cousins with enjoyable donkey rides. And this must be my pleasure today.

Small boys could not manage everything on their own, it was difficult to get unaided onto Nancy's back and so the help of Uncle Oswald was sought. He, perhaps a little reluctantly because important work was in hand, agreed to give us five minutes.

In far less time than that, a set of harness was brought from the saddle-room. The harness was much too large for Nancy, but she stood reasonably still while the outsize in leather drapery was attached to her head and buckled onto her back. When all was complete, Nancy stood dejectedly in a pair of blinkers which obscured a large part of her face on either side.

"Cum on then, young Ken, if yer wants a ride," said Uncle Oswald. "Don't fret, 'ers as quiet as a mouse." And I was hoisted, splay-legged, up onto the far too spacious saddle.

It would be an understatement to say that I felt at ease. Rather were my puny muscles tensed to retain a position in the centre of the polished leather. There was no hope that my feet would reach the stirrups, loose dangling below, and I was compelled to adopt the posture of a professional jockey to retain balance. So with arched back and fingers in Nancy's mane, I awaited events.

But nothing happened. Uncle Oswald attempted to provoke Nancy into forward movement by exerting thrust at a point near the bit in her mouth but Nancy just twisted back her ears and the bit slipped out over her nose. In fact, it soon became clear that Nancy had no intention of moving from the place where she stood. Even when my cousins added their weight to her hindquarters she remained stubbornly static.

I am quite certain that she would not have capitulated had not Charlie Markie thrown an empty milk-bucket on to the stone-paved floor just behind us.

This caused my cousins to somersault, Uncle Oswald to lose his hold on the rein and me to bite the end of my tongue.

As for Nancy, she made several leaps with hind legs kicking, first to one side and then to the other, so that the saddle became a thing convulsed. I shall never know how I retained my seat because the donkey intended otherwise. It was just beginner's luck that I was still on Nancy's back when she broke into a canter and then into a trot. Finally, she came to a standstill in the corner of the yard but not before turning to face her adversaries. By this time my head was almost shaken from my shoulders and my arms were in a state of collapse.

I am quite certain that my uncle and cousins were prepared to continue with my first donkey ride but I had absolutely no enthusiasm for further involvement. Accordingly, I was lifted by Uncle Oswald back to the ground where I stood awhile in a most unsteady condition.

Basil gladly took my place. No sooner was he well seated in the saddle than his expertise was revealed to us all. He jerked his body rapidly backwards and forwards making 'checking' noises and, at the same time, he dug his heels into the donkey's flanks. It all looked most professional, but once again Nancy refused to move. Her twitching ears and resentful stare indicating an inborn opposition to persons clambering about on her back.

However, she had not calculated on Uncle Oswald's next move. Mindful of the donkey's fear of sudden noises in the rear, my uncle picked up the milk-bucket. He did not throw it down onto the paving as before, but rattled it by the handle just behind Nancy's tail.

This had an immediate result. Nancy commenced to trot around the yard with Basil in command on the saddle, Uncle Oswald and the bucket in close pursuit.

But there was quite an unexpected turn of events.

Mr Cull, his face wreathed in smiles, looked over the farm-yard gate and ejaculated, "Wat's the caper then Mister Oswald. Collectin' manure fer the rhubarb?"

Roars of laughter were heard in the cow-stalls as Uncle Oswald returned, somewhat bashfully, to continue the milk-ing. The harness was taken back to the saddle-room and Nancy, still motionless, awaited her bovine sisters. Soon she would return with them to the meadows, glad to be relieved of the unsolicited encroachment recently endured.

For my cousins and I, the day was now fast drawing to a close. A period spent sliding down the straw in a partly-filled bay in the Dutch barn and then to the farm kitchen. Here a slice of bread and butter and a mug of cocoa and finally up the stairs to our ample bedroom.

This dormitory was by no means lavishly furnished. Two double bedsteads with iron rails and brass knobs. Plain scrubbed timber flooring with a home-made woollen rug along-side each bed. A wash-stand with a marble top supporting a large earthenware bowl and jug. Underneath two chamber-pots with handles, all adorned with a blue and white decoration.

The windows had no curtains, but this was of little import because the room was not overlooked. There was an upright chair with a wicker seat at the side of each bed and on one of these was placed an enamel candlestick.

Scant attention had been paid to decoration as the ceiling was brush-marked white with lime and a green distemper had been applied to the walls. The rather barren atmosphere was somewhat relieved by pictures which hung above each bed. Both had religious texts and each exhorted my cousins to be good boys.

As was the custom, we slept in our shirts. Each left his outer clothing surmounting his boots and we clambered into bed. Ronnie and I together, Basil on his own. The candle was blown out and for awhile its aroma lingered, then, as the darkness transformed to pale moonlight, we settled easily into our feathered bedding and soon fell asleep.

Next morning we awoke very early but, even so, the farmyard was already alive with noise and movement. My cousins and I did not remain long in bed. Rather was this a good time for wrestling. Ronnie and Basil, it would seem, normally started the day in this manner and no exception was made to routine because a guest was present. Indeed, I was welcome to pit my strength if I so wished. It appeared that the invitation was a courteous gesture and need not be taken too seriously. Ronnie and Basil required this method of self-expression. Ronnie, because he was twelve months senior and had to establish his superiority and Basil, because of his short-fall, wishing to prove that age had no import.

I think it is true to say that Ronnie normally succeeded in retaining the advantage which the age-gap afforded but the challenge was serious and must not be taken lightly. And so for fully ten minutes two scantily clad small boys rolled over and over on one of the bedsteads, panting and grunting. Only when Aunt Edith arrived in the room did the contest terminate.

"Hurry up and make your beds," she said "and come down to breakfast. I can't hang about this mornin', I've got a lot 'ov washin' to do."

We did as we were instructed — but first we must wash. Ronnie poured a limited amount of water from the large jug into the basin and we took it in turns to moisten our faces with a small square of towelling to which we first applied some soap. The cold water did not stimulate a lengthy exposure and when each of us had made a paltry gesture, the water was poured into one of the chamber-pots.

Next the pillows had to be straightened and the sheets and blankets pulled over them, then we stumped our way down the wooden staircase to the kitchen where three boiled eggs were waiting to be eaten.

To follow, and as a special treat, we were given a small bowl of cornflakes, further enriched with cream from the top of a seventeen gallon milk-churn, and sprinkled with brown sugar. Never before had I sampled this delicious dish. I was not in the least surprised when Aunt Edith told me it was what the angels ate. Furthermore, if I had it for breakfast every morning I should be able to leap over five-barred gates, just like Sunny Jim on the Force packet. But I remember that I decided that I would not want to wear a top hat without a brim, nor have my hair done up in a pigtail which stuck out at the back.

Soon after breakfast it was time to take the milk to the canal. Here it would be collected by Cadbury's long-boat to be transported to their Frampton-on-Severn factory.

When the final bucket had been tipped into the cooler and its contents had trickled down into the churn, a careful check was made of the quantity. This was a job which Uncle Oswald reserved for himself. Nobody else could be trusted to carry out such an involved operation which had financial significance. There was adding up to do, a record-book to fill in and a counter-slip to pull out. All very complicated.

Several churns held milk produced from the evening yield and now there was the morning's milk to add on.

When all was done, six churns were hoisted onto a four-wheeled porter's trolley and we set off down the drive.

It was a noisy and bumpy journey. The iron wheels of the trolley jumped about on the loose gravel and the churns clattered and gyrated in accompaniment. I had grave fear that a churn might fall over, but past experience had shown my elders that this did not happen. So they propelled the unsteady vehicle with a reckless abandon, from time to time shouting to my cousins and myself above the metallic clamour. We understood little of what was said and even less of the supporting gesticulations.

Our journey was broken at the 'black-shed' where a stop was made to feed the calves in the yard. Whilst most other wildlife had vanished, they at least had no fear of the noisy cavalcade and they bawled their approval through the tarred railings.

Tom Davis wasted no time attending to their appetites and, clambering back over the gate, he was soon involved in our clamorous progression.

Shortly afterwards we reached Castle Bridge, but not before

Castle Bridge.   [Michael Edmonds]

considerable pushing up the steep pitch onto the canal bank. When we stopped all was peaceful.

My eyes absorbed the tranquil scene which was Gloucester's way to the sea. A vivid impression of a mile of placid water, extending in two directions, bisecting the green countryside like a long glass window. I stood for a while transfixed. The abrupt tranquillity, now that the noise was gone, accentuated the serenity so that it made an indelible picture in my mind.

My eyes followed the path of water, neat bordered in green, until it shimmered and merged into a sun-hazy distance. Half as far stood a grey heron, his legs obscured by a clump of rush, and nearer still a herring gull 'cauked' from the top of a tall post. A white butterfly made an erratic crossing close to the water and I was fearful lest it might fall in before reaching the patch of nettles where it ultimately settled. In a meadow, near at hand, stood a stately oak and under its shady branches, brown and white cows flicked their tails.

When I looked towards Gloucester there was something new which held my attention. As yet a quarter of a mile away and coming towards me, I saw a long black boat. A man on the towpath was leading a horse which strained the end of a long rope well secured to a post near the prow. In the stern another figure pushed a pole attached to the rudder hard towards the bank. With collective effort the long-boat retained an easy walking pace and it grew larger minute by minute.

This was the milk-boat — Cadbury's milk-boat — and in steady time it would take to Frampton the yield of the Parkend cows.

Day after day, through foul weather and fine, the churns of milk were transported. Today's shipment was but one in an endless succession without a break.

Full ten minutes passed before the long-boat arrived with us, but in less time than this, as was the fashion in the country, a loud conversation had started with the crew. We knew very quickly how many gallons had been collected from The Pilot Bridge and the quantity picked up at The Stank. It would soon be possible to compare the Parish of Hardwicke's contribution with that of Moreton Valence, as there was some rivalry in this matter.

What perhaps affected Ronnie, Basil and myself far more was the be told that the Hardwicke gluttons had not eaten all the lump chocolate with which the crew had started its journey. There would be some available for us when the long-boat got a little nearer.

Anticipation prolongs time, so it is said, and I well remember that my mouth was watering before the long-boat crunched against the tarred timber staging where we waited.

Only then did we receive our chocolate. A large lump was thrown to each of us and although mine rolled about on the gravel bank before I recovered it, I still found the flavour magnificent. It mattered little that the pleasant tasting morsel was in no condition for sale in the shops. Chocolate in this form went from Frampton to Bournville where it became confection. Here on the canal bank it tasted just as good.

It did not take long to hoist the churns on board. Powerful brown arms swung each tapering container onto the gunwale and with no arrest in movement, other arms propelled it down into the well of the boat. In even less time an equivalent number of empty churns were rocketed ashore and a quota of these took their place on the Parkend Lodge Farm's 'porter's trolley'. Hardly had the last metallic rattle died away when a stout pole was pushing the long-boar out into mid-stream again.

During the exchange of cargo, the pony had enjoyed a short-term meal of grass, but this equine pleasure was rudely terminated by the tow-path carter's demand for a further long haul. The brave animal responded with arching back and muscle-rippling legs which dug iron shoes into the gravel. A snort accompanied each powerful tread and the taut hemp tow-rope twanged a little as it slipped fractionally through the anchor-ring. Ripples appeared in the smooth water at the prow as the tar-black hulk slid forward and the journey to Frampton was resumed.

My cousins and I stood watching and we returned the fare-wells which were waved to us by the crew as the long-boat glided away. Even the grown-ups were prepared for involve-ment and they engaged in comic banter until the crew was well out of earshot. Voices carried across the water and a good five minutes elapsed before it was no longer possible for a caustic quip to register. No useful purpose would now be served by further long-distance dialogue so Uncle Oswald said, "Cum on then, let's git baak to th' faarm."

We were on the point of doing just this when Tom Davis, his voice bubbling with excitement, shouted "Yer cums th' Ruth." We all looked in the direction of his gesticulating arm and saw, coming up to a bend in the canal and still a very long distance away, a form which appeared larger than life. Without doubt it was a ship but as yet it appeared to be moving slowly across open meadowland and it dwarfed the trees which stood near it.

The oxide hull looked like a rusty cathedral and above this was a white superstructure holed with many windows. Funnel, masts and derricks pointed to the sky.

Tom had seen this ship make her way to Gloucester Docks several days previously. Now she was destined for the open sea again. But first she must make the laborious journey back to

Sharpness and the sixteen miles would leave little change from the day.

I was very glad when Uncle Oswald decided that we should wait for a closer view and so we sat down on the grass with our eyes glued on the slow moving merchant-ship.

I had not previously noticed a black-and-white funnel which was moving some distance in front of the large vessel but now, on rounding a bend in the canal, I was afforded my first view of the tug which was hauling her. The little grey boat hugged the outside bank and then slackened effort allowing her captor to negotiate the bend under her own momentum.

At last the great nose came into view. Inch by inch it lengthened until half the towering hull was in sight. Then, when the prow was almost probing the far bank, the busy tug again took command, but now pulling at an angle from a central station. Steadily the great ship straightened towards us and soon we were looking, endways on, at the majestic lady and her fussy little dog on its lead.

Progress was slow and minutes passed before it was possible to measure advance, but gradually the distance between 'Ruth' and Castle Bridge grew less. At long range, movement could not be detected while the ship came directly towards us.

Progress became more obvious when the grey heron, all in safe distance, took wing. Several arching flaps carried the large bird above a mature oak and it continued its departure along the line of a drainage rean across the water-meadows. At the same time, two crows left the oak but it was the heron and not the Ruth which provoked their flight, for they cawed fiercely as they gave chase. For a while we watched this aerial contest. The black birds dived aggressively at the larger grey one which, in turn, proved to them that the sky was full of empty spaces!

When we looked back again, 'Ruth' was appreciably closer to us. Besides the powerful rope which connected her to the tug, we could now see that there were two further ropes stretching across the water to the tow-path, one from the prow and one from the stern. In either case were men involved. On board, the rope was attached to a winch, while ashore, a looped end could be placed over a bollard. At regular intervals of a few yards, the tow-path was dotted with these anchorages, and the men who were responsible for the looped ends moved forward on foot, bollard by bollard. If the 'Ruth' deviated from her course, then this was corrected by the winch winding in at prow and stern.

Thus steadily she progressed until less than a hundred yards separated her from Castle Bridge. Then, once again, the tug slackened and the 'Ruth' reversed her propeller. Speed was reduced to almost standstill, men shouted to each other and bells rang.

Long before this time, the two halves of Castle Bridge had been swung around to reveal a gap between the stonework which appeared insufficiently wide.

How could so great a bulk as 'Ruth' get through? Surely we were about to witness calamity. As if in anticipation, the menfolk got to their feet and my cousins and I followed suit.

"Stan baac, ther's good bhoys," said Uncle Oswald, brushing us away from the water, but never for a moment taking his eyes from the oxide hull, growing more gigantic each second that passed.

"Ers a whooper ther's no doubt!"

Slowly, so slowly 'Ruth' inched her way forward and we noticed men with ropes to which were attached balls of hemp, leaning over the gunwale.

"Them's te cushon the bump," explained Uncle Oswald to three hypnotized juveniles now gripping each other by the hand.

With barely a ripple in the water, the tug glided slowly between the two halves of Castle Bridge and, as she passed us, we heard the thumps of her engine now idling in her bowels, the heavy tow-rope trailing in the water like a black serpent.

"Er's the 'Mayflower'," explained Uncle Oswald as a man on deck, with a broad grin, gave us a 'thumbs-up' signal. At least **he** did not appear to be unduly worried.

Inch by inch the massive prow of 'Ruth', towering above us,

Cadburys Factory forms the backcloth of this photograph as the 'Mayflower' follows the 'Severn Stream' through Fretherne Bridge, Saul.

[Courtesy S. F. Birch]

came closer, dividing the water between the bridge into two equal halves.

Although the surface was still, down below there was turmoil, indicated by a patch of rush which swirled, first one way and then the other. Man-made steel plates were now compressing thousands of gallons of water. Some must go through the bridge and some escape to the rear.

The space between the stonework gradually filled with metal until only a few inches of gap remained on either side. So accurate was the work of the pilot on the bridge that the balls of hemp had no contact with the stonework. As 'Ruth' slid safely through the narrow passage they were hoisted back on board.

When all was clear, 'Mayflower's' engines trundled actively and the slack in the tow-rope steadily disappeared.

And, once again, the mighty 'Ruth' was under way to the open sea.

The two halves of Castle Bridge were swung back into place, one by Mr Holder, the local bridgeman, and the other by a man on a bicycle who rode the tow-path the full sixteen miles for the purpose.

Just as soon as road contact was resumed, sundry pairs of wheels, held up by 'Ruth', passed over the canal. As indeed did several pairs of country legs. Six from Oakey Farm.

100

Four of these legs rushed at me and the woolly body which they supported pushed me flat onto my back. Then a long moist tongue slobbered the side of my face as I attempted to protect myself. It was indeed Bear , the Old English Sheepdog. And with him came Uncle Percy.

Fortunately for me, Bear s enthusiasm to make friends was generalised over the whole Parkend contingent and seconds later cousin Basil was also on his back. I am sure that Ronnie would have suffered the same fate had not Uncle Percy hooked a finger in Bear's collar and belted his haunches with the flat of his other hand.

Basil and I got up from the ground and Bear sat down, whimpering resentment for what he considered grossly unfair chastisement. Several times, when he thought Uncle Percy was 'off his guard', did Bear make a sudden leap in our direction, but Uncle Percy's strong finger held him. Ultimately Bear accepted captivity grudgingly by stretching full-length on the ground, almost pulling my Uncle's arm out of joint in the process. It is perhaps superfluous to say that Bear was a very large dog. He was indeed just that.

However, it was not until many summers had passed that I learned how Bear had obtained his name, but it will not be out-of-place to tell this now.

It appears that one of the Parkend folk, who for obvious reasons shall be nameless, was walking through the meadows with his lady-friend. As the evening wore on, they sat themselves down on a grassy bank. Shortly afterwards a mist commenced to rise. Things began to get interesting when, suddenly, a large hairy animal appeared out of the fog, at the top of the bank above the couple. The male, in recounting the incident to a close friend, is reputed to have said, "Wen 'e cum, I thaught fust of all, twer a grizzly bear, then I seed twer only Pussy Prout's bloody dawg."

It goes without saying that the name Bear remained with the Old English Sheepdog for the rest of his days.

Today, as a comparative puppy, Bear was still a frightening creature, particularly to small boys who were his inferior in weight and size. I think that Bear knew this fact and took a measure of playful satisfaction from the dominance he held over us. Just when we thought he was prepared to be submissive and would tolerate a measure of fondling, Bear would suddenly decide that the best place for small boys was on their backs and would ensure that he put us into that position as quickly as possible. It was useless even to run away because, in speed also, Bear was our master. For years to come, he would continue to exercise this superiority. Now he lay, full length, a massive woollen rug, making snorting noises periodically and snapping at the odd wasp which had the audacity to disturb him.

Uncle Percy, while still keeping a watchful eye on Bear , soon became involved in serious conversation with the other grown-ups. This allowed my cousins and I to steal up onto the bridge. From this elevated position we had an even better view of the canal in either direction. Ruth was now half-a-mile nearer Sharpness, but, passing her where the canal was widest, was yet another boat. For a moment we watched, but quickly our excitement overflowed and we were compelled to share the dramatic news, so we ran back to the grown-ups shouting "Ther's another boat a'comin'."

However, our wild enthusiasm had little effect on them as they barely condescended to look where we were pointing. Their attitude was summed up by Tom Davis, who said rather languidly, "That's only th' 'Wave'."

But to us it was yet another ship. Maybe not as large as 'Ruth'. Perhaps even a lot smaller, but a ship nevertheless and now coming quite rapidly towards us.

The only grown-up who appeared in the slightest interested was Mr Holder who was again walking down the bank from his house. My cousins, of course, knew Mr Holder and were soon asking him "Can we 'av a ride, then?"

"Yes bhoys, ye kin 'av a ride, but kip still an' kip away fram th' rails."

Such an invitation needed no second bidding and I followed my two cousins who darted back up onto the bridge.

My cousins knew exactly where to stand because they had done it all before and I took my place between them.

"Hole tight then bhoys," shouted Mr Holder when he was satisfied that we were standing a yard removed from the joint between the two halves of the bridge. Then he lifted a hook achored to a stout post which held a ring securely fastened to the massive square pole. Bending down, he comfortably positioned the rounded end of the pole between his shoulder and neck, hung his right arm over it before leaning his whole body to exert maximum pressure sideways. As the massive timber structure began to move slowly around on its circle of little iron wheels, I experienced a feeling of instability.

Looking back at the bridgeman, I saw that his body had become almost parallel with the ground, his russet face now balanced on the pole and his heavy boots shuffling, inch by inch, the well worn arching path. Making two-thirds of the quarter circle, Mr Holder regained an upright position and allowed the bridge to complete the remaining third under its own momentum. Just the right amount of effort had been expended to bring half the mobile timber bridge parallel with the bank.

When all was still, I looked again at 'Wave' and found that she had glided appreciably closer. From either side of her prow

The 'Wave' passes through Frampton bridge with a good complement of passengers on a summer's day in 1914. [Courtesy B. L. H. Shaw]

stretched a furrow of water diagonally backwards to each bank. This collected the bright light of the sun and oscillated the bullrush. A whisp of smoke escaped above the black band on her otherwise red funnel. On her superstructure were rows of well-painted, sparsely occupied slatted seats. A figure in blue serge and white-trimmed naval cap had control in the wheelhouse.

This indeed was 'Wave' and, with her sister ship, 'Lapwing', she plied daily the full length of the Sharpness canal, carrying the county merchandise to market and its people to Gloucester's shops.

Suddenly, Ronnie had a bright idea, "Let's zee if th' swaller's got eggs," he said excitedly as the thought flashed in his mind. He jumped down from the bridge, deliberately tumbled onto his knees and then rolled on the grass underneath the timbering which was normally over the water. Basil and I followed automatically; neither was prepared to miss any new adventure. Boats could wait and, in any event, this swallow nest would only remain available while the bridge was open.

In the heavy shade I did not see immediately all that was above me. But as my eyes became accustomed to the poor light, I saw large black beams and smaller black beams which crossed above them. A mine of timbering without coal. But a coal mine indeed!

Taking his body weight on his left elbow, Ronnie's right arm stretched upwards, his hand probing a small grey corrugated basin of mud.

"Er's got vive," he told us.

Now to me this was completely artificial. That a bird should nest under a bridge and use mud as a building material just did not make sense. I was not prepared to accept such unusual conditions without a thorough investigation. So I crawled closer to see for myself.

In the space of the next few second my preconceptions of nesting pattern took a rude shock. There was, without doubt, a bird's nest and it could not have been produced by Ronnie himself in so short a time. While the basin was made with mud, the nest which it contained was soft. White poultry feathers and fronds of spongy grass were the bed-clothes. In this snug environment and partly covered, was a ring of little white eggs with warm brown spots.

My thieving fingers could not resist the temptation and almost immediately one of the eggs was warm in my clammy hand. Had there been the slightest thought that the egg might be returned to the nest then the opportunity moved away above me with the closing of the bridge. My conscience was clear, how was I to know?

But I now had a swallow egg. White with warm brown spots!

My cousins and I did not need to move to return to the sunshine. Mr Holder saw to that. Soon we were sitting upright watching the stern of 'Wave' moving away in a turmoil of boiling water.

Now there was a general exodus. The passengers from the boat, loaded with luggage, tramped wearily away. Percy Prout and 'Bear' headed the long straight road to Oakey Farm. The Parkend trolley with its attendant party commenced its noisy return journey. And soon Castle Bridge was left to a serene peacefulness and the watchful gull on a post.

The Prout Family: Uncle Oswald, Ronnie, Eileen, Aunt Edith and Basil.
[Courtesy Mrs E. Tranter]

Chapter eight
A nest of hornets

The next morning, after a liberal helping of angel's food, my cousins and I were again seeking agreeable occupation. Many things of agricultural consequence were available for our indulgence but little consideration was necessary to make a choice. We would go with Cecil Hewer to the blacksmith's forge at Hardwicke.

But while things were being prepared for the trip, we could well fill in our time pumping water for the milk cooler. It was very obvious that my cousins carried out this commitment grudgingly and regarded the time spent in filling the tank in the attic as poor occupation. It was not exactly hard work but it demanded static concentration. No small boy could remain happily in one place for long periods of time.

But an order was an order and a trip in the 'buggy' might be refused if we complained. So we took it in turns to wrench the handle, up and down, until water from the 'tell-tale' overflow pipe signalled that further drudgery was not required of us.

"They'm learnin' disciplin'," said my uncle to my aunt. Then he turned to us, satisfaction written all over his face, and said, "Cecil's ready fer yer in th' stable, an' mind no foolin' about!"

We needed no second bidding. Whooping and yelling, skipping and jumping, we careered down the drive to secure our places in the 'buggy'.

On arrival, we found that all preparations had been made. The pony was harnessed and standing alert in the shafts, while behind, a much larger animal was secured by a halter-rope to

106

the back of the 'buggy'. Doublet was his name and he was destined to receive a new set of shoes. It was hardly likely that Doublet was aware of what the future had in store but he resented his attachment to the back of the vehicle and he exposed a measure of apprehension by shuffling his feet in a nervous manner.

I could never quite understand why the Prout family found it necessary to christen every horse with a name beginning with the letter 'D' and when I raised the question with either of my uncles I could not obtain a satisfactory answer.

"They de jus loike te be kalled Duke or Duchess or Dublett or Diamond or summat beginnin' with a 'D' or summat."

And there the matter was always dropped!

"Get in steddy then!" said Cecil with a measure of annoyance in his voice. "Fer gawd's sake quieten dawn a bit. You'll 'av us all in a heep in th' bottom ov ther trap if yer done mind out!"

Maybe we thought it best to take notice of Cecil's request or perhaps the expectation of what was to come brought a measure of silence. Be it as it may, now we sat quietly awaiting Uncle Oswald's permission to make our departure.

After a few words of instruction to Cecil he gave his blessing, "Git along then, mine 'ow ye go on th' main rode, an' done be laite!"

Parkend Lane was now familiar country and as we travelled slowly between its two splendid hedgerows I was able to establish the exact location of the gateway leading into Oswald Prout's wide and fertile fields. There was an occasional larch and two mature spruce sheltering the lane. Eighty yards away, mid-field, a majestic oak spread its mighty, leafy arms over a bunch of Gloucestershire cattle flicking their white tails. A clump of tall white poplars formed a corner coppice with the Bristol road and here a kestrel winnowed momentarily in the summer sunshine.

Cecil, obviously now quite relaxed, commenced to whistle, perhaps slightly out of tune, "Pack up your troubles in yer old kit bag."

Climbing a slight pitch, we turned left onto the main road and headed in the direction of Gloucester.

Traffic was light but when an occasional vehicle made contact with us, the horses acknowledged each other by sluvvering their nostrils and swivelling their ears.

We passed the end of Parkend Covert and soon, away to our left, stood the noble facade of Hardwicke Court. Farm animals browsed in the intervening parkland.

Then there appeared 'The Cross Keys Inn', standing astride the Bath and Bristol roads, and finally our destination — the Hardwicke Smithy.

A red-brick building with slated roof, having windows with several broken panes. Single storey, yet commodious, surrounded with an array of metal-work which rusted for want of use and indeed for need of repair.

Oss-raikes, zide-raikes and tedders, mowers, reapers and binders. They were accumulated erratically and would be titivated all in good time, as the seasons demanded.

Many items of agricultural equipment had overflowed across the road and were stock-piled around a wooden shed with a Roman-tile roof.

The smithy on the corner of Haresfield Lane, Hardwicke.   [Courtesy Mrs S. Davis]

The whole area surrounding the smithy was clad with a crunchy covering of dark blue-grey ash, best traversed in hob-nailed boots.

Our cavalcade came to a rather unsteady halt following a vociferous "Whoah" blared by Cecil. This sudden impulsion had its effect both inside and outside the smithy. Inside all work stopped temporarily, and outside Doublet came, head and shoulders, into the rear end of the 'buggy', almost tipping Cecil onto the floor.

For a few moments I was separated from my two cousins by a hairy grey wall which impressed me warmly against the padding on the back of my seat. Relief came when Cecil turned and shouted "Git baack" at the same time punching Doublet's nostrils so that he blinked and snorted his displeasure.

As soon as space was available I escaped to the ground and was joined by my cousins at the rear end of Doublet. Here we waited while Cecil untied the knot in the halter which secured him to the back of the 'buggy'.

Once free, Doublet was led through the now open doorway into the smithy and he was followed by three apprehensive yet enquiring young country ruffians.

Although outside the sun was shining, it was by no means bright as day inside. The main source of light was the wide open doorway. The several broken windows were clad internally with black smoky sack-cloth so that they contributed little to the general illumination. But compensating to some extent, a warm red glow was emitted by the open cinder fire which fluctuated in intensity as air was breathed from a bellows. A smoky atmosphere charged with this comfortable glow permeated the whole interior.

Figures, almost in silhouette, moved, devil-like, and there was a continuous clanking noise which penetrated my ears. Only when the eyes became accustomed, did the interior convey full impact.

There stood the smith himself, a fine figure of development, with bulging arm muscles, distorted by excessive use. A long leather apron, almost reaching the ground, which concealed an ample belly. A pair of steel-rimmed glasses perched on the end of a bulbous red nose and a bare shining head which looked polished in the sweaty glow.

Strips of metal, held by long tongs were pushed into the whitest part of the fire. Then they were hammered on the anvil and ultimately they were doused in a container of water.

Dexterity fashioned by years of experience produced the shoe that fitted perfectly the horse's hoof. Then the smith hammered it into place, the horse's foreleg held firmly between his knees, with little regard for personal safety. It was all so manfully industrious and it gave me my first insight into the fabrication of metal. My exodus from the tender age of ineptitude. Now was I being baptised.

Doublet was surprisingly submissive. I now suspect that the man in the leather apron provided some form of magical affinity which Doublet trusted. The horse lifted his legs when the smith jerked his chubby fingers through the long greasy hair and he stood silently while nails were driven into the undersides of his hoofs.

"Cum on me bhoy, Oi bent a-goin te 'urt ee," said the smith and Doublet really believed him.

When all was complete, the smith stood away, the backs of his hands clipping his waist, while Doublet shuffled his feet as a human trying on a new pair of boots.

My cousins and I had not completely wasted our time for now each of us had discovered a discarded horse-shoe. Mine I held at arm's length so that the smith might give his blessing.

"Auld 'im up th' rite way, bhoy, or the luk will run out!" I was told and at the same time my hand was turned so that the open-ends pointed skywards.

"That's it, keep 'im jus' loike that an' you'll be aulright!"

The instruction was clearly understood. The horse-shoe must remain for all time as the smith had directed, no matter what the embarrassment. In future one hand only was available, even for personal commitment. And so, with some difficulty, I ascended the steep metal step back into the 'buggy'. Once on board, my problem was less difficult but after a while the pony's jerking motion made my arm begin to ache. So I must use two hands and support the weight on my thighs.

Cecil glanced at me and smiled to himself.

Long before we reached Parkend Lodge Farm the problem had become unbearable and when the 'buggy' came to a stand-still I was quite unable to raise my arms.

I had no alternative but to sit still and wait for assistance. This came in time from Aunt Edith who took the horse-shoe from my now numbed fingers and set it down on the kitchen window-sill without spilling its fortunate content.

"Oh, you lucky bhoy," she said.

The next day we had visitors. An uncle and aunt and three more cousins. All the way from Malswick Farm near Newent. A little over twelve miles in a pony and trap. They would stay for mid-day dinner and not return home until late in the after-noon. Another Uncle Percy, not to be confused with the one from Oakey Farm, and my mother's sister, Aunt Annie.

Perhaps what concerned me most was that two of the cousins were boys and their ages fitted well with Ronnie, Basil and myself.

Uncle Percy had spent his boyhood in a parish near Stroud and maybe it was no coincidence that he should have sons called Stanley and Leonard. Albeit, Stanley came first but of course he was the King. King Stanley or Leonard Stanley, each was an adjoining parish, anyway.

For a few hours there would now be five male cousins at Parkend and a team of that size must surely find every bird's nest in the district.

So we set out along the lane with Jack and Spider, the two Parkend dogs, to help in the search.

It was a fine sunny day, warm and still. A trickle of crystal clear water bubbling in the well overgrown ditch competed with the hum of a fat queen bee. The hawthorn was in full flower and its lace-like bloom yielded a sweet perfume to the clean, still air.

By this time I had become sublimely rural and, like my four

cousins, I wore a pair of heavy hob-nailed boots. Our clothes were similar also, short trousers of rough tweed with jacket to match and thick grey woollen stockings. Only our caps were different, but school counted for nothing on a day such as this.

The loose chippings on the lane crunched with our heavy footwear and our excited voices, competing with each other, added to the din. Hardly the conditions for successful oology, but Stanley soon took command.

"If yer de wan' ter vind birrds nests, then ver gawd's zake less noise," he instructed. "Let's 'ave one on eche zide of both th' 'edges, an' Basil cun walk up th' ditch iv ee as th' mind. Beat with yer sticks an' watch wat vlies out."

Surely no waiting gunner could have wished a more intensive scouring. It was unlikely that any occupied nest would escape detection.

Soon a hen blackbird, in her sooty brown livery, chack-chacked away in a frenzied splutter of annoyance. Ronnie pushed his head into the prickly bush from whence she departed, dislodging his cap in the process and catching his ear on an offending thorn.

"Er got vour," he said. "Very normal. Any'won want?" he further enquired. There were no takers so the greenish eggs freckled with brown remained for the blackbird's return.

A song thrush, followed by a further blackbird and then a hedge sparrow flushed as we progressed, but no eggs were taken as neither offered abnormality.

Then, from a frail nest made with dead stems and suspended in a straggling bramble, departed a little grey bird which none of us clearly saw. We gathered around to inspect where Leonard pointed with his stick.

"It's a warrbler ov zorts," said Ronnie. "Tom Davis got an egg jus' loike them."

It was now my turn to look. I lifted a bramble leaf with my finger and there, sheltering beneath, loosely constructed and yet compact, was a flimsy net of gossamer holding five stupendous eggs. Never before had I seen anything so wonderful.

An egg was carefully removed from the nest for closer

112

examination. Stanley and Ronnie held a profound discussion and then came to the unanimous conclusion — ''They be nettle creepers,'' they said. And the rest of us took their word.

Each cousin, in turn, removed an egg from the nest. My prize I carefully deposited in an 'England's Glory' matchbox lined with sheep's wool removed from a barbed-wire fence.

And the hunt continued.

The hedges on each side of the lane were slashed without mercy. My cousins attempted to out-do each other believing that the violence of their strokes alone produced a successful flushing. The two Parkend dogs, provoked by the thrashing cacophony, dashed in and out of the bushy tangle, every moment expecting some wild animal would break cover. They were certain that only a lurking badger or fox would justify such a concerted onslaught and each attempted to be present at the point of departure when the creature bolted. Leaves and sticks flew in all directions as turmoil overtook the otherwise tranquil countryside.

A wood pigeon, frightful of the advancing holocaust, departed from a tall thick blackthorn, leaving two white heavily incubated eggs. These were tested in the water below and confirmed as unblowable, so that the parent bird would later return to continue her brooding.

The black twig platform of her nest, a little disarranged by Stanley's full-stretched arm, was pushed back with a stick into a level position.

It was not without interest to me that both eggs popped to the surface of the water in the ditch. Not before had I seen an egg which could float and I reluctantly accepted Stanley's diagnosis — ''They'm bent any good te thee, Ken. Thees' 'il never blo' 'em. They'm too var zet!''

I was further disappointed when a little brown bird flitted away in front of me, its wings buzzing like a fat tawny bee, as it vanished into the thick of a blossomed hawthorn.

''Did yer zee that Jinny Wren?'' enquired my cousin. '' 'Er nest is just yer, but 'ers got young.''

I scrambled up the bank to investigate. At first I could see nothing and then my cousin's stick pointed to a small bundle of dead leaves. Round like a withered cabbage with a tiny hole in the side. With a little trepidation, I inserted a finger and the writhing warmth of the feathery interior confirmed my cousin's diagnosis.

Next a robin slipped away from an earthy cavity in a rotten willow stump. Once again there were dead leaves in profusion with a neat lining of animal hair. The partly fledged young were clearly visible in the scraggy basin-shaped nest. With beaks wide open, the baby birds gyrated their necks and, in the half-light of the cavity, they appeared as yellow tulips writhing in a breeze. All the while the mother bird, partly tame, flitted from twig to twig, close at hand.

Soon she, in turn, was able to go back to her nest as the band of noisy hunters moved away.

A further twenty yards and then another tawny bird slipped out from a grassy bank. I was quite close to the spot from which the bird departed. I saw clearly its yellowish head as it disappeared into a thick tangle of thorn and goose-grass and, what was more important, I found the nest itself without help from my cousins. However, I had to rely on Ronnie's expert knowledge to identify the treasure.

"You've vound a scribblin' schoolmaster an' ers for vour!" he said excitedly.

The cousins gathered round and peered into the soft grassy bunting nest lined with rootlets, where rested the four creamy-pink eggs spluttered and scrawled with brownish markings.

Yes indeed, the judderings of a bizarre school don. 'Scribblin'' was with doubt an apt description, for the surface markings were just that.

Now came the problem. There were five cousins and only four eggs. Someone was going to be unlucky.

What was to happen? Should we toss up? Nobody had a coin, anyway. So Stanley said, "I vote Ken 'as an egg, he found th' nest."

Now if I felt like objecting, my desire to possess did not permit me to speak and I was more than relieved when Ronnie said, " 'Im as found 'as fust call.''

And so into the 'England's Glory' matchbox went the first of the treasures and I felt a terrific pride of possession.

Stanley, with an eye to protecting his family interest now made the suggestion that seniority should have priority for the remaining eggs. This meant that he, his brother Leonard and Ronnie would each be fortunate while Basil, the youngest of the five cousins, would go empty handed.

This formula almost reached unanimous approval and had only one objector, Basil, who unfortunately for him, was in a minority of one.

Accordingly, his watery eyes watched with envy the three remaining eggs disappear into three boxes other than his own and, with a gulp in his throat and head hanging low, he shuffled his way on up the middle of the ditch.

But fate plays funny tricks and the day was still young. The rather strained atmosphere was relieved by a hen-pheasant which shot out from the grass near Ronnie's boot. The sudden cacophony arrested all human movement and we stood watching the bird's rapid departure up the hedge and across the adjoining field. Her rapid wing movement alternating with long glides propelled her at great speed and she shouted her disapproval as an accompaniment. A long rasping rattle of noise.

She had departed from a nest containing fourteen glossy, khaki-coloured eggs, just smaller than those we had eaten for breakfast and almost as warm.

The eggs were in two layers. Four on top of ten, with dead bents and a few feathers intermixed. The top four eggs were removed, one by one, Basil's extraction leaving a space in the lower layer. Death by shooting, later in the year, was accordingly reduced by a potential one-third, but we must say nothing of this to Uncle Oswald.

We had pressed on a full thirty yards before further ornithological contact was established and now Basil had his revenge. A bird, brownish and nearly as big as a song thrush, had left a ragged, grassy nest in the middle of a hawthorn.

Now my youngest cousin was crawling under the bush to

lay first claim. Not deterred by scratches on face and limb, he probed his fingers into the nest and extracted the only egg it contained, which was his by right — a 'Butcher-Bird' had provided Basil with the greatest prize of the day.

He led the way back to Parkend Lodge Farm with a smile of deep satisfaction on his face and a jewel which neither of us could match in his pocket.

The following day I had my first meeting with Jim. An association which continued, pleasantly for us both, until he left this earth well past his eightieth birthday. But on this day, in my childhood, there is just one more story to relate. And tell it I must.

Jim Browning was a salmon-fisherman and he lived at Elmore on the banks of the Severn river. In every way a true countryman, toiling on the water and on the land.

Uncle Oswald was expecting visitors from Hardwicke and a salmon was needed to feed them. Who better than Jim to provide it? So once again the Parkend 'buggy' left the farm, but this time it was Uncle Oswald himself who held the reins.

When we crossed Castle Bridge I was in 'virgin territory', 'breaking new ground' and 'pioneering the true vale'.

The road to Epney village was flat and open to the sky. Close-cropped hedges on either side with pollarded willows hugging the ditches. The peewits tumbling over the meadows all the time uttering the sad call denoting their name and a solitary snipe drumming diagonally downwards to the tussocks or rush and sedge. It was indeed swampy country in those far distant days.

He who would walk the water-meadows in leaking boots must needs get wet feet. At first glance, to those unsuspecting, just a grassy pasture, but footprints fast water filled by any who would penetrate.

Short of 'The Anchor Inn' on the river bank the 'buggy' forked hard to the right and soon Epney was left behind.

Longney, with its scattered farms and red-brick cottages, found a mellow sweetness in my enquiring eyes. I could have travelled on for ever and a day.

But soon, over the parish boundary into Elmore and almost in sight of its church, we were at Jim's wooden two-roomed bungalow. Slab stone steps led up the steep bank from the lane to a rustic timber gate, painted dark green. A gravel path led us through a neat garden of lawn and rambler roses. Over the front door grew a honeysuckle and there were two wooden steps.

A deep Gloster voice from inside said, "Cum on in, no need ter knock!"

I was not the first to enter but when I did I was frightened by what I saw. It was Jim Browning. Sitting in an easy chair, his head balanced on a white pillow. His face appeared to be twice the normal size and all-over very red. One eye was completely closed and the other nearly so.

"I've bin potched tree times by they 'ot-footed varmints," explained Jim and, when Uncle Oswald enquired for further particulars, Jim said, "No, not waps, they darned 'ornets!"

Jim then went on to tell us the story.

He had been working on a ditching contract for the Water Board with his mate, Porky Phillips.

Porky, as I later found from personal contact, was a simple countryman. Getting on in years yet still capable of a hard day's work. Silver hair on a massive bronzed chest protruding through an open flannel shirt. Sandy corduroy trousers, hitched well up at the knees with 'bagging-string'. Well exposed hob-nail boots, grey for the lack of polish and a large disk of exposed brown skin on top on an otherwise grey hairy head.

When Jim and Porky reached a group of three pollarded willows growing over the rean they found that the first tree was host to a strong nest of hornets.

The steady drone of swarms of these black-and-gold tyrants convinced them that this was not the correct time to continue operations under the trees. They best leave off for thirty yards and work on the other side of the trees. Come back well after sun-down, when the hornets had gone to bed, and finish the dangerous section.

117

This was agreed and acted upon.

Well into the evening, the two ditch-diggers and Jim's liver-and-white spaniel dog, Punch, returned to the willows.

There was no movement, all was quiet.

The two men started digging where they had left off earlier in the day. Full shovels of sloppy black ooze began to pile up on the banks on either side of the ditch and, gradually, the most dangerous point was reached — immediately below the hollow willow.

Suddenly there was pandemonium.

Porky slipped as he swung around and his shovel hit the trunk of the willow. An internal drone commenced in the tree and upwards of a dozen hornets buzzed out.

The ditch-diggers lost no time in making their escape. Jim turned away and made a rapid departure down the ditch, while Porky scrambled up the bank and ran as fast as he could into the open meadow.

It was Porky who attracted the hornets and he swiped desperately at them as they buzzed around his head. He holloed loudly as the attacks were pressed home.

Jim, now a safe distance away, was greatly amused and he burst into laughter. He had never seen Porky move so fast in all his life. Neither had Punch, who had been sniffing for rabbits in the corner of the field.

It was now the dog's turn to join in the fun. He raced after Porky who stumbled and fell headlong as the spaniel caught up with him. The swarm of hornets now took a keen interest in Punch. The dog was stung at least one, he yelped, and ran, tail between his legs, with the swarm still in attendance, to the safety of his master.

It was now Jim's turn to run for his life and he did this by scrambling up the bank furthest away from the fast approaching dog and then bolting into the adjoining meadow.

But it was all in vain. Punch soon caught up with Jim, so did the hornets and the ditch below the three willows still remained undug!

Chapter nine
Bowling for a pig

The 'buggy' ride to Elmore was fully justified. It produced a very positive result. Not one salmon but two. Both 'botchers'. One a little over seven pounds and the other just under nine. "Some zixteen pounds ov darn gued grub ter line the bellies of the' 'elpers aader the 'ardwicke fête.''

A supper was to be provided at Parkend Lodge Farm as a mark of appreciation, such was Uncle Oswald's good nature, but much of the hard work must fall on Aunt Edith and Daisy Brooks in the kitchen. There would be several days to prepare and Saturday would accommodate the great event.

When the day arrived my cousins and I received a thorough personal examination before departure for the fête was permitted. Our faces must shine like our boots and our jackets and trousers must be brushed clean.

"You mustn't be a bad advertisement, all the parish will be there," we were told as flannel and brush were applied with vigour. Only when our elders were completely satisfied were we allowed to join the large party which was going on foot across the fields to Hardwicke Court.

Once clear of the farm buildings, Ronnie, Basil and I ran on in front and we were soon many yards ahead of our chattering elders. Talk of fashion, of satin, of taffeta and of lace did not interest us. Rabbits were more 'up-our-street', and there were plenty of them in Parkend Covert, two fields in front.

Just how we were to catch the rabbits we really had not thought, but we could at least make several hundred run for their lives, and that would be exciting.

The last white tail had flicked out of sight well before we

reached the wood and here we paused a short while before opening the hunting-gate which led us into the shadow of many massive oaks.

A grey squirrel leapt in the branches, a jay 'quarked' loudly and there was a steady hum of insects. Light filtered through the leaves overhead which rustled in a slight breeze and, below our boots, the ground was soft.

I had never seen a squirrel before, nor had I heard a jay 'quark'. What else would happen in this new, strange and exciting environment?

We had not long to wait, because as we stood silently watching, a badger came trundling down the pathway towards us. Nose to the ground, he was oblivious of the three humans rooted twenty yards away.

I glanced at my cousins. They stood wide-eyed with looks of apprehension on their faces. A badger in the wild was obviously new to them.

Brock continued his slow forward movement, all the while probing the dead leaves and soil with his snout, veering to each side in turn, and making soft piggy noises which emphasized his satisfaction.

Only when he was a 'field-gate' away did the badger react to us. Our scent reached his nostrils and he suddenly became alert to danger. Slowly his body rose until it assumed the posture of a begging dog, and he stared solidly at us, his nostrils twitching inquisitively.

My cousins and I stood, frozen to the ground. Was the badger about to attack? The hair on the back of my head began to tingle.

But Brock had no such vicious intent. Maybe he did not trust any human, but nevertheless, he was curious to know what three young ones were up to in his wood.

For a full half-minute the badger surveyed us and then, satisfied that we intended him no harm, he sank back into a bovine position and continued rooting for grubs. He advanced no further towards us but, very leisurely, he ambled away at ninety degrees to our left.

120

I was about to move forward when Basil grabbed me by the arm and, at the same time, Ronnie cautiously pointed down the woodland track. There, coming towards us, was another badger. This one slightly smaller than the first. She was round and plump and her body was nearer the ground. Her black-and-white striped head was held low and her nostrils snuffled in the dead leaves.

As though enacting a similar routine to her mate, she advanced to the same spot where he performed his 'begging-trick' and she, in turn, sat up and looked at us. Unlike him, however, she overbalanced twice before following her husband into a blackthorn thicket.

This exciting experience was graphically recounted to the Parkend Party which soon caught up with us. I question whether our elders were prepared to believe one half of what we told them about our meeting with the badgers. Although in no way admitting the fact, I am confident that Aunt Edith thought our story an exaggeration for she said, "Old Leighton-Ridgway 'as a couple ov black-an'-white cats, an they de 'unt rabbits in the wood. Maybe that's wat you d' see."

Tom Davis, however, provided us with some credence when he said, "I've 'urd tell of badgers a'standin' on ther 'ind legs afore!"

The discussion on badgers continued unabated while we tramped along the spongy path through the wood, but once through the hunting-gate on the Hardwicke side, there were other things to capture our attention.

Soft music wafted impulsively to us and, away in the distance, we could see the tops of several white canvas tents. As we drew nearer we heard, from time to time, a strange rumbling sound and, occasionally, there was a peal of laughter. Obviously we were all going to enjoy ourselves and so we hurried along to join the madding country-crowd.

Soon we stood before the fine stately home of the Hardwicke Squire and all around us were stalls, tents and tables. There were people everywhere and a lot more people were coming down the drive from the Bristol road. Smiling faces, raising hats and handshakes by the dozen. A chatter of voices which surged alternately with the intermittent rumble.

By now I was becoming curious. Just what was making this strange noise which, quite often, was followed by cheering voices? I questioned my cousins and was told, "They'm a' bowlin' fer th' pig. Let's go an' zee!"

We made our way rapidly in the direction of the rumble and soon came in sight of the skittle-alley. This consisted of a close-boarded wooden platform some six feet wide and twenty yards long. At one end a diamond of nine wooden pins, each a foot high, and down the side a sloping trough in which the three balls were returned to the bowlers.

"A tanner a go," was the order of the day.

For this princely sum, the three balls were hurled, in turn, at the nine pins and, if by chance only two were necessary to clear the board, then the watching crowd shouted "Spare" and the bowler qualified to take part in the 'play-off'.

The winner would take home with him the small pig which squealed from time to time in a nearby pen and was then allowed to suck milk from a bottle, thanks to the kind-hearted little girl in a pink frilly dress.

My cousins had seen this all before but to me it was a new experience and I stood wide-eyed while, one after another, the local menfolk exposed their prowess.

They stripped off their jackets and — those who were wearing them — ties and collars. They rolled up their sleeves, exposing hairy arms browned by the sun. Then they hurled the wooden balls at lightening speed, as if to split the pins in pieces, believing, no doubt, that a thunderbolt was more likely devastate than a much slower missile.

Occasionally, through lack of strength, an older man would bowl a slower ball and the pins would fall in equal numbers!

A potent desire to come out on top existed in many of the participants, but there was obviously a more personal rivalry which demanded the laying of side-bets.

In any event, business was very brisk. 'Tanners' flowed into a tin box at one end and the two 'stickers' panted sweat-fully at the other.

Then Uncle Oswald and his friend, Bill Barnes, from Gloucester appeared. It was obvious that they intended bowling for the pig, for they both stripped off their jackets and placed them with their trilby hats on the ground.

My uncle won the toss. His first ball missed the front pin by a quarter of an inch and went right through without touching the ones behind. The second ball hit the front pin full-square and took the middle and back pin right out. Left with an impossible frame, the third ball accounted for two pins on the right and five only was Uncle Oswald's score.

Now it was Bill Barnes' turn. His first ball ran slick along the boards, hit the front pin just at the right angle and the 'stickers' cleared seven fallen pins from the frame. Two adjoining pins only remained and Bill Barnes' second ball was just as accurate, both fell and everyone shouted "Spare".

A city-dweller had joined the élite and his name was recorded on paper for the bowl-off much later in the day.

My cousins and I now made contact with Uncle Oswald and his successful friend whose good fortune stimulated the purchase of lemonade and buns from a stall close at hand. Until then, we had wondered just how we would obtain these delicacies with no money in our pockets. Bill Barnes had now become our hero and we told him how well he had bowled!

For several hours which followed we went the rounds of the fête. We inspected all the stalls, had a ride on a pony and dipped our arms in the bran-tub. We tried our luck at 'hoop-la', whizzed through the air on the swings and were given a coconut by Tom Davis, which he had won but did not want.

"I'de loike 'em alrite, but they de' get stuck in a bad tooth which makes yer vase 'urt summat awful."

We were introduced to the Vicar, who patted each of us on the head. "Good boys, I'm sure," he said with benevolence!

But all too soon was the day drawing to a close. The assembled company was making its way to the skittle-alley for the final bowl-off between those who had obtained 'spares'

"Won ball eche ter vinish yer 'and an' then us 'ill zee if a vurther play-off be needed,'' everyone was informed.

One ball was all that was necessary to settle the matter. When it came to Bill Barnes' turn, seven skittles fell exactly as before and, as neither of the other players was able to equal or improve on this number, he had won the pig.

"What bist thee a-goin' ter do we 'im, then?'' enquired Uncle Oswald. And when Bill Barnes indicated that he had absolutely no idea, Uncle Oswald continued, "Theese best let I taak 'im back ter Parken' an' kip 'im until 'ee be grow a bit.''

This proposal appeared quite attractive to Bill Barnes; a formula to defray the cost of feeding the piglet was worked out and transport to the farm was arranged.

Tom Davis would go back across the fields, harness the pony, then drive round the road to the Court. The piglet would be perfectly safe in the 'buggy' when the door at the back was closed and my two cousins. as fellow-travellers, would ensure that it would remain in a placid state on the floor.

When the time came, I was also permitted to ride back to Parkend and the journey was by no means devoid of amuse-ment. The piglet, unaccustomed to the lurching movement of the pony-trap, insisted in pushing itself between our legs and the seats. Just when we thought that it had settled it-self comfortably, it would squeal, its trotters would scrape the floor rapidly, and it would then push itself behind yet another pair of our legs. On a number of occasions I found it necessary to straighten my stockings which were frequently pushed around and out of place.

The piglet squealed several times when we were passing another horse-drawn vehicle. The surprised look on watching faces indicated the belief that three small boys were making rude noises. "Disgustin','' I heard one old lady say as her countenance soured.

But, in spite of all the problems, we arrived safely at our destination, the piglet was provided with a comfortable straw-filled sty and christened with the name 'Skittles' by the young country bumpkins whose job it would now be to feed him.

The story of the piglet had a codicil which was enacted over the next several months and it would not be inappropriate to continue to explain it now.

Bill Barnes was now stimulated to make frequent visits to Parkend Lodge Farm, if only to see for himself the progress in development being made by his pig.

There was much good humoured banter at the time of such visits on the part of the 'grown-ups', each attempting to out-do the other in subtle 'leg-pull'.

"Yer be pig-varmer Barnes," would be Uncle Oswald's welcome.

"Ow's my stock then, bailiff?" would be the visitor's enquiry.

And so the tittle-tattle would continue.

"Theese gentle-men varmers do wan' ter zee their stok vrom time ter time, I'll be bound."

"We der need ter watch they slick varm managers," would be the reply.

One day Uncle Oswald sent a message to Bill Barnes' office in Gloucester.

"Please tell 'im 'is pig's got swine-vever!"

Initially the impact of this news was profound. In fact it produced the effect that Uncle Oswald intended. But as time progressed, Bill Barnes became more and more convinced that this was yet one more 'leg-pull'.

How then was he to counter this latest intrigue? Then he hit upon the answer.

He had a telephone conversation with his friend, Archie Houston, a veterinary surgeon employed by the Ministry of Agriculture, from whom he obtained particulars of the procedure required in such cases. He then telephoned Sergeant Barnfield at Hardwicke Police Station, a much respected and good-hearted friend of the Prout family, who agreed to participate in the farce.

Within the space of the next hour, Sergeant Barnfield rode his bicycle to Parkend Lodge Farm where he informed Uncle Oswald that a Swine Fever outbreak had been reported to him by Mr Bill Barnes and accordingly it was necessary for a

125

quarantine notice to be issued. Sergeant Barnfield was therefore issuing the notice forthwith.

Uncle Oswald remonstrated that the Swine Fever outbreak was all a practical joke and that the pig was perfectly healthy. He was informed forcibly that the matter was now in the hands of the Ministry of Agriculture and that there was nothing more the Sergeant could do about it.

Working strictly to the time schedule previously arranged by the conspirators, an hour later Archie Houston arrived at the farm.

He was at pains to find out where the dead pig had been buried as it was necessary to send part of the intestine to the laboratory for critical examination. Without this procedure and confirmation that the pig had died of the disease, the quarantine notice must continue indefinitely.

All the problems of the outbreak were exposed and gravely explained in detail. There could now be no retraction.

Only when a complete impasse had been reached did Bill Barnes time a jocular entry.

"A good job twer not Foot and Mouth Disease," he exclaimed, and Unce Oswald's anxieties were relieved with roars of laughter.

Chapter ten
'On the boat' to G'oucester'

I awoke early the next day because I had been told that I was to go to Gloucester 'on the boat'. This would be a thrilling experience. I had heard the grown-ups talking about going by water to Gloucester; now I was to do just this.

Aunt Edith had decided that Ronnie needed a new pair of trousers and Basil a new pair of boots so to Gloucester we must go. Ken could hardly be left on his own at the farm so he could "cum fer the ride".

We had porridge and a fried egg for breakfast, then we set off down the lane to Castle Bridge.

It was a bright and sunny morning. A hare loped along in front of us, sat up on its hind legs twitching its whiskers and then it bolted through the hedge having decided that humans were not to be trusted.

We found two further expectant passengers waiting at the bridge. They were Aunt Minnie and Miss Shepherd from Oakey Farm. Aunt Edith gasped up the final slope to the water and the country ladies were lost in earnest conversation.

Ronnie, Basil and I were left to toss stones into the placid water.

Today the 'Lapwing' would carry us to the Gloucester shops but, as yet, she was not in sight. She was slightly smaller than her sister ship, the 'Wave', but just as sprightly.

Mr Holder wandered down the tow-path towards us. He had plenty of time to reach the bridge before the 'Lapwing' arrived but he was anxious to share in the ladies' conversation and equally to keep an eye on three young country bumpkins who might do some damage to canal company property.

At last the 'Lapwing' appeared around the slight bend at Moor Farm but, as yet, she was half-a-mile away. Steadily she came towards us, but some minutes passed before Castle Bridge opened to receive her. Then there was great activity. Engine throbbed, bells rang and men shouted. Baggage and parcels passed from ship to shore and from shore to ship. In turn we were all helped on board by a brown hairy arm.

And then we glided on our way.

To me it was a thrilling experience. Never before had I travelled in so smooth a manner. Journeys in the 'buggy', on the milk-trolley and even on the train were noisy and full of vibration. Now I moved forward faster than I could run without the slightest shake.

'Lapwing's' prow made diagonal waves which slopped hollow cavities in the bank where her forward moving hulk had sucked water to her stern. Patches of rush were embroiled in the tornado.

A kingfisher flashed its bright metallic plumage, green and blue, as it skimmed the water and then was lost as it darted below the tow-path. A moorhen, with jerking neck, took flight, momentarily dragging its legs through the water as it rose. Another grey gull cawked from a post.

A slight bend in the canal and we were in view of the Stank Bridge. Here the surrounding countryside was higher and we were leaving the water-meadows of Oakey and Laynes Farms. 'Lapwing' was entering Hardwicke parish.

She slackened speed long before she reached the bridge and was without movement before I realised what was happening. It was to allow a tug and a chain of barges to pass. These vessels had been hidden from my view by the masonry supporting the bridge. Now the grey tug with her black-and-white funnel was moving steadily towards us through the gap in the stonework. She was the 'Speedwell', a sister ship of 'Mayflower'. Indeed, most of the tugs plying the Sharpness Canal bore the name of a flower.

In a short time I was to learn that a majority of the barges that carried the merchandise were given the name of a

The 'Speedwell' and 'Hazel' tow the grain carrier 'Harriet' towards Gloucester just after the First World War.   [Courtesy Mrs A. G. Harrison]

Gloucester district. There was the 'Barnwood', the 'Brockworth' and the 'Tuffley'. These three were now approaching us, roped behind the tug and there were two 'long-boats' in the rear. They had probably carried timber to Gloucester Docks to the order of Joseph Griggs, Price-Walker or Nicks & Co. Now empty, they moved steadily back to Sharpness for more. As each in turn passed slowly by, the man at the stern waved an arm.

When all was clear, 'Lapwing' and 'Speedwell' exchanged two short friendly hoots and then engines started to thump again.

A hundred yards separated us from the landing-stage where two country-wives joined the jovial company already on board. My aunts and Miss Shepherd lost no time in making contact with the newcomers and they were in turn joined by Paul Francillon who, I was told, was a very important person. In fact he owned the 'Lapwing'! What a fortunate man!

We had not travelled very far before we saw a row of fishermen with rods stretching over the water. They did not appear to be particularly pleased to see us as they lifted their lines from the water. No doubt the tug and its barges had caused a long period of water disturbance. Now, just when things were settling down, 'Lapwing' was producing another upheaval. However, this time it was only one boat. It would soon pass and tranquillity would return.

Then came the Pilot Bridge, which took its name from the public house which overlooked it — or did the brewery decide to name the inn to comply with its neighbour? In any event, both bridge and pub were respected and the word 'Pilot' was integral to Hardwicke village.

Here there were more passengers bound for Gloucester. They included Mrs Webb and her three daughters, Kathleen, Jessie and Ruth. It was very fortunate that Uncle Robert was not on board as I am sure that I should have paid a heavy penalty. Three lovely country-girls, all about my own age. Uncle Robert would have been in his element!

Then there was Harry Barnes. At present a handy-man working for Farmer Webb. Known to all the customers of The Pilot Inn as Harry, with a surname added to denote that he slept rough in a barn belonging to any farmer who employed him. He had brought a crate of oven-ready Light Sussex from Hardwicke Farm which Mrs Webb would be selling in Gloucester. When 'Lapwing' departed he would be free to 'have a pint' before returning to feed the pigs.

There were three more bridges we must pass before reaching Gloucester Docks, but the next was the most important. The Lower Rea Bridge collected passengers and merchandise from Stonebench, Elmore and Weir Green. There were a number of people from each awaiting us. When all was on board, very few vacant seats remained around 'Lapwing's' gunnels and there was a steady hum of conversation coming from below deck.

The man in his wheel-house rang a bell, thumps responded and we were again on our way.

Upper Rea Bridge was passed without a change in our cargo and soon we were moving up the 'long-straight' parallel with the Bristol road.

It was here that we met a rowing boat. I had never seen one like it before. My cousins told me it was a racing boat and that they were to be seen at the Castle Reach Regatta every year. It was long and narrow. It held five men, four with long oars. It appeared very much overloaded. 'Lapwing' thought so too as she slackened speed to allow the shallow craft to pass. Having shouted their appreciation, the men in the racing boat strained every muscle to show how fast they could leave us. In, out, in, out, in, out, instructed the man holding the rudder-ropes, and the oars kept meticulously in time.

I was soon to know a little more about boat racing as in a short while we were passing the Gloucester Rowing Club. This was a large building constructed mainly of timber and painted white. It stood a few yards away from the water's edge. It held racks of boats of many sizes for 'sculls', 'pairs' and 'foursomes'. As we passed, another racing-craft was being brought down to the water and men in white shorts and singlets with red-and-black squared edges were doing the lifting. Gladly, I would have remained for a while but 'Lapwing's' propeller was again in motion and the two halves of Hempsted Bridge awaited our passage.

Now we were passing the sprawling timber yards. Stacks and stacks of this ubiquitous material awaiting the demand of the building trade. Most of this timber had found its way by canal from Sharpness and now gangs of men were busy loading it into wagons for delivery by road. It was heavy work and vast quantities of beer were consumed by the men, many of whom were stripped to the waist.

As we proceeded, the timber-yards, with their scattered gaunt repositories, were replaced by congested brick ware-houses, some five storeys high. There were flour mills and factories, oil stores and builders' merchants, food stores and ship chandlers.

This was Gloucester Docks and I was making my first contact with an environment where I would be required to spend a great deal of my time in the many years still to come.

When 'Lapwing' was roped securely to her appointed place, the entire company of passengers filed ashore. They formed a temporary crowd on the quay and then moved away in small

Gloucester Docks at the turn of the century.

parties towards Southgate Street.

Aunt Edith appeared to be in such a hurry to get into the centre of things that my cousins and I had great difficulty in keeping up with her. With panting breath she told us that Uncle Martin and Aunt Lizzie were coming into Gloucester by pony and trap and she wished to catch them at the hostelry before they walked up into town. Fortunately, for my cousins and I, we were less than a quarter of a mile from the inn and we arrived concurrently with Aunt Edith.

There was quite a lot of activity in the spacious yard. Two men were pushing a trap into line with some others and a man was leading a pony into a row of stabling where a number of these animals were already tethered. This was the manner in which the farmers of the day parked their conveyances and all journeys to market by pony and trap had this commitment before the auction sales were reached on foot.

Many a farmer, having imbibed an excessive amount of alcohol, would stagger back to the hostelry and then be assisted into his pony and trap. The faithful pony would take him home even though the farmer was quite incapable of finding his way. What present-day motor car would be capable of doing this or indeed avoid a charge of driving while under the influence of drink!

Aunt Edith, after making enquiry, discovered that my Haresfield relatives had already left for the town centre and so we ourselves made our way up Southgate Street.

It was not long before we reached Rolfe & Morgan's 'Golden Anchor' clothing shop and it was here that Ronnie's trousers were purchased. A considerable number of pairs were inspected and prices negotiated before a decision was ultimately reached. Lennard's shoe shop was then visited and here similar long-term scrutiny took place before Basil's boots were purchased at least a half size too large to accommodate his future growth.

It was now the turn of the grocers, Sterry & Morris, and here only a small amount of food was collected by my aunt because the bulk of the family's requirements would be delivered as was the custom in that more practical day.

The principal reason for our visit to Gloucester was now discharged and we were able to 'look-around-the-shops'. Mr Pope's Bon Marche was first on the list, then Wallace Harris' music shop, followed by Ward & Woodman, the chemists. Pickfords for a tin of paint, Parsons for a packet of screws and Blinkhorns for some curtain material.

We were walking up Eastgate Street towards the Cross when a farmer's wife emerged in a great hurry from Botherway's eating-house. She was large, had a bun of hair on the back of her head and wore a long pleated skirt which almost reached the ground.

She charged into the middle of the street, cupped her hands to her mouth and shouted at the top of her voice, "Hoi!" She was attempting to attract the attention of some children walking away, opposite Brunswick Road.

Everybody in Eastgate Street stood still, including two small boys in front of us.

Then I was privileged to hear the finest illustration of Gloucestershire dialect as one boy turned to the other and with a smile on his face, said, "Er bent a'callin' we, us don't belong ter shee."

The farmer's wife, having attracted the attention of her

Easgate Street, Gloucester. [Courtesy Mrs P. Jones]

children, hurried off down Eastgate Street to join them and the rest of the curious pedestrians within earshot resumed their normal routine. My aunt decided that it was time we had a snack and so my cousins and I were ushered through Botherway's framed glass door and seated at a table which had a top of small green ceramic tiles.

A cup of tea and a large Chelsea bun was consumed by each of us and then we started on our way to the Cattle Market. Our progress, however, was impeded by five bullocks which came racing up Eastgate Street towards us. They were being driven from Clarence Street into Brunswick Road but the animals had decided to change their route and had galloped by the drover standing in the middle of the street.

The problem was soon resolved by a number of the visiting country-folk who stepped fearlessly from the pavements forming a cordon through which the cattle were not allowed to pass. They were turned and then driven back the way they had come but not before they had splattered manure over Blinkhorn's shop windows.

This episode was in no way exceptional. Cattle and sheep were driven freely through the streets of Gloucester on Mondays and Saturdays and shopkeepers expected to have cleaning up to do as a result. Pigs, being less easy to drive, were normally transported by wagon!

When Aunt Edith was satisfied that it was safe to proceed and the bullocks had disappeared down Brunswick Road, we continued our walk into Clarence Street and then Market Parade.

Here was the Mecca of the North Gloucestershire farmer. He came even though he might have nothing to buy or sell. In any case it was desirable that he should know the value of things. Were prices rising or falling? When was the right time for him to buy another milking-cow or sell six of his tegs? Proximity to the auctioneer on sale day could give him the answer and Bruton Knowles and Pearce Pope were well suited in this respect.

Today the auction was nearly over and some animals were already making an exodus. Drovers were being hired by the purchasing farmers to marshal new stock to their farms. These drovers were hardy men in tattered clothes and hob-nailed boots. They would walk many miles for a few shillings and maybe a pint of cider before they returned to their poor lodgings.

This was the pattern of things as animals bawled, baad and squealed and a steam of sweat rose from them into the plane trees whose branches forked overhead.

We walked along the avenues between the rows of animal pens examining the livestock and talking to the owners. Then we went into that part of the market set aside for the 'cheap-jacks'. Here Aunt Edith bought three pairs of leather boot-laces and a dozen candles.

Pressure was exerted on my aunt to buy a great deal more but she avoided the artful approaches made to her with professional abandon.

Time was now fast approaching when we must 'catch-the-boat', and so we retraced out steps to the canal. But not before we had been bought a bag of 'humbugs' to suck on the way home.

And so it was, in those far away times, little pleasures were sweet!

Two views of the old Cattle Market just after the First World War.
[Both courtesy Mrs P. Jones]

Chapter eleven
Apple-pie beds

A pleasant surprise was awaiting our return to Parkend Lodge Farm. My aunt had said nothing of the matter. Maybe she had not herself been informed. But sitting on chairs in the kitchen, supping tea, were two voluptuous girls, who were nieces of my aunt.

These charming young ladies lived a long distance away and we had never previously had contact with them. Aunt Edith had, however, stressed how wonderful were the children of her brother and what a pity it was that Ronnie and Basil did not emulate them.

It is probable that my cousins had become conditioned to this periodic ejaculation on the part of their mother as they now exposed an attitude of subservience to their newly found female relatives. This atmosphere certainly permeated its influence on me and I regarded the girls with a measure of unmitigated awe. The girls had aristocratic voices and spoke to us with condescension. We were three country bumpkins and we should be treated as such.

This condition was maintained until we were packed off upstairs. Then the spell was broken. We had 'apple-pie' beds!

"The ruddy perishers," exclaimed Ronnie, the first of us to discover that his feet could not reach their rightful place. Then it was Basil whose movement into the sheets was arrested half-way.

There was no alternative than the remaking of our beds and this procedure was carried out in our scant clothing with a whistling cold draught to chill our buttocks.

"We must get our own back," said Ronnie, "I'll think ov summat."

By morning Ronnie had made his plan and this was put into operation late in the afternoon when the girls were away on a country walk.

The wardrobe in the 'spare-room' occupied by the girls was emptied of my aunt's clothes and a liberal covering of newspaper was laid inside the door. Then, three broody hens were taken from the fowl-house and placed in the wardrobe and the door was closed.

Now Ronnie said, "Stand quiet an' listen." We did just this and we were surprised by the queer noises which emitted from the oaken cupboard at frequent intervals. Beak chattering, feather ruffling and an occasional subdued 'squaak'.

"That should do the trick," said my cousin. "Now we tell them gals ther's rats in the 'ouse."

At an appropriate time when none of our elders was present the information was passed on to the two young female visitors, who appeared to show little concern that they would be involved in any way. Ultimately, the time came for 'going-to-bed' and as soon as the girls were safely installed in their 'spare-room' we crept along the passage and took up station outside their bedroom door.

We kept very quiet and waited for an indication that our plot was having success. But no such indication came and ultimately when it became abundantly clear that the girls were fast asleep we returned disconsolately to our own room.

Our plan had misfired!

All that remained for us to do was to return the three broody hens to the fowl-house, clear up the well-fouled newspaper and replace Aunt Edith's clothes. We were fortunate in carrying out all three commitments without detection during the following morning.

But Ronnie was not prepared to give up. "I've got another plan which 'ill give em 'emp," he said. Then he revealed an elaborate scheme which we immediately put into action.

A large ball of 'bagging-string' was taken from a cupboard in the kitchen and a good ten yards was cut from it. Then we quietly entered the girls' bedroom.

Immediately below a window stood a mahogany night-commode. Ronnie raised the lid and tied the end of the 'bagging-string' around the chamber-pot. The he stood on a chair and threaded the string up behind the velvet curtains and over the four-inch mahogany curtain pole. Then the string was passed out through the window.

By tying the end of the string to a kidney-bean stick, Ronnie was able to pass it to Basil now standing at our bedroom window. From this position, by a gentle jerking of the string, the chamber-pot rattled inside the mahogany night-commode.

We were now ready for action.

At last night came and once again we retired to our bedrooms.

We had planned the procedure very carefully: Basil would remain in our bedroom and would operate the string, Ronnie would stand outside the 'spare-room' door, and I was instructed to convey Ronnie's instructions to Basil, soft-footed along the passage. No action was to be taken until we assumed that the girls were in bed.

For quite a long time the female visitors were talking and moving about and this caused us to become somewhat impatient. There was a risk that one of the young ladies might come out into the passage, en route to the toilet and so discover us outside the door. But visits to the toilet were normally made before persons went upstairs to bed.

"Urry up, you perishers," hised Ronnie anxiously, "I wants to get things moovin'."

At long last Ronnie was satisfied that the girls were in bed and I was dispatched to tell Basil to start jerking the 'bagging-string'.

When I returned I found Ronnie with his ear to the keyhole. "I can't yer nothin'," he whispered. "Tell Basil to jerk 'un more."

So I retraced my steps and conveyed the instruction. On two further occasions I was directed to inform Basil to increase movement as no reaction was apparent from the 'spare-room'.

Then, suddenly, there was an unholy crash. The lid of the

night-commode flew open, the chamber-pot sprang into the air and the curtains and the mahogany pole crashed to the floor.

Both girls screamed.

For quite a while Parkend Lodge Farm was in a state of pandemonium. We boys had a great deal to answer for, particularly as one of the young ladies had wet the bed.

We learnt some while afterwards that Ronnie's plan had succeeded right from the beginning. The chamber-pot had rattled from the first tug of the bagging-string and that our female visitors were terrified because the curtains started to move as well!

There were two residents at Parkend Lodge Farm who lost no time in befriending me. Maybe I possessed the correct canine aroma or just had the right appearance. I shall never know, but as so many dogs have since shown, Jack and Spider took me right from my first contact with them. They were both collies and they worked on the farm herding cattle and sheep.

Jack was the older by several years and to denote this fact his coat was various shades of grey. He had a white patch on his chest and underparts and he had a stumpy tail which had, in part, been removed when Jack was a puppy.

Spider was sandy. Brown sand on his back, light sand in the middle and no sand at all on his underparts. Spider had a conventional and normal length tail.

It was perhaps Jack who showed me the greater affection. He followed me everywhere and never failed to fondle me should I sit down or relax.

The dogs spent the night-time hours in the shed where the animal cake was kept. They had two separate straw-filled boxes which they went to without hesitation when the Prout family retired to bed. They were let out early in the morning and then raced upstairs to our bedroom to ensure that we did not oversleep!

My cousins and I dived under the bedclothes as soon as we heard the noise of the dogs' paws on the wooden stairway.

The door would burst open and the two hairy monsters would hurl themselves at us, pleasantly growling their satisfaction. When all their nightly conserve of energy had been used up, Jack and Spider would snuggle down in our beds.

Jack normally selected me as his companion and he would lick any exposed part of my anatomy before snorting and shuffling into a comfortable position, just like a broody hen.

Jack and Spider were working-dogs and they fully understood what was required of them at milking time. Not only did they assist Uncle Oswald and his cowmen to bring the animals into the farmyard, but they were capable of doing this alone if Uncle decided.

It was not unusual for uncle to allow the milking-cows to have access to several grazing fields during the daytime and confine the animals to one only after evening milking. Gates were therefore left open and Jack and Spider would bring the cows in without human assistance if instruction was given them.

"Go an' fetch 'em," was the order shouted at the gate to the farmyard and the dogs did the rest, all on their own!

Jack and Spider were good at doing other things too. Not the least of these was rabbiting.

The dogs appeared to understand each other and they worked together as a team. One dog would crouch its painful way in a thick thorn hedge and the other would wait outside for the quarry to bolt. Then the next time they would change positions. It was almost as though they said to each other, "Now it's your turn to get scratched."

Maybe Spider was the more effective in chasing the bolting rabbit since his longer tail assisted a quicker turn as the quarry darted first one way and then the other.

There were splendid places for rabbiting at Parkend Lodge Farm. Parkend Covert, the middle oak and the wood-pile were some of the best, but whichever place you chose the adage, 'A rabbit in the quat is worth ten in the burrow' remains perfectly true.

It was not long after my adventurous stay at Parkend Lodge

Farm that I returned to Standish. Perhaps a few days or maybe a couple of weeks elapsed. After sixty odd years, I do not remember. It is perhaps sufficient to say that in my young life I made many visits to Moreton Valence.

Standish Court was my base camp but I sojourned at various other farms of my relatives in the northern part of my native county.

In the early days I travelled to them on steam train or pony and trap. Ten years later it was by bus or on a bicycle. Silvey's bus to Saul, Davis' bus to Newent and the Blue Taxi bus to Moreton Valence.

They were carefree days of cider and Double Gloucester cheese. Days when the sun was the clock and firewood the fuel. When the pump was worked by tawny arms and grass was cut with a scythe.

It is sad that those days are now gone for ever and even the memory of them will die with my generation.

I am glad I lived when I did and I am thankful to all those who befriended me during my span of living.

Acknowledgements

I would like to thank all the kind people who have helped me so willingly with this book, especially Roy Counsell. Also my niece, Rachel Beckingham, who very kindly designed and painted the cover illustration. I am deeply grateful to a number of good friends for assistance and advice in writing this book and my thanks must be placed on record to those who allowed me to reproduce their photographs and illustrations. The Editor and staff of The Citizen newspaper have afforded unstinting help and expertise and much of the credit for ultimate publication is due to these knowledgeable persons.

K. D. P. Pickford